Spreadsheet Templates for

Production and
Operations Management

Jay Nathan
University of Pennsylvania at Clarion

James R. Evans
University of Cincinnati

Ronald J. Grambo
University of Scranton

West Publishing Company
St. Paul New York Los Angeles San Francisco

COPYRIGHT © 1990   by WEST PUBLISHING CO.
50 W. Kellogg Boulevard
P.O. Box 64526
St. Paul, MN 55164-1003

97 96 95 94 93 92 91 90   8 7 6 5 4 3 2 1 0

ISBN 0-314-70497-3

TO OUR CHILDREN

Shyam and Shila
Kristin and Lauren
Erin and Mark

TABLE OF CONTENTS

PREFACE

The resurgence of interest in production/operations managment (P/OM) as an important functional area of business is due to a number of factors: global competition; the availability of new managerial tools such as MRP, JIT, and CIM; increased concern about the quality and reliability of products and services; and the awareness that operations management can be an effective tool for competitive strategy. Teaching production and operations management can be a challenging and rewarding experience for instructors. The purpose of this workbook and spreadsheet template software is to enrich the educational process for P/OM and to make the teaching and learning of the concepts, tools, and ideas of P/OM more effective and enjoyable.

This new and revised workbook and software are the product of careful design and critical evaluation and review by students. The templates have a dynamic expansion capability that allows any reasonable size problem to be solved from menu-driven commands. P/OM educators will find spreadsheets to be a useful tool for solving problems and cases, particularly using "what if" simulation of various scenarios.

We thank our editors, Dick Fenton and Esther Craig, and others at West Publishing Company for their continued support throughout this project. Finally, we hope that the user will find the SPREADSHEET TEMPLATES FOR PRODUCTION AND OPERATIONS MANAGEMENT to be an enjoyable and valuable addition to the study of production and operations management.

Jay Nathan
James R. Evans
Ronald J. Grambo

Chapter 1
INTRODUCTION

This chapter provides an overview of the hardware and software requirements for using Spreadsheet Templates for Production and Operations Management, and essential LOTUS 1-2-3 concepts needed to use the software effectively. It is not intended to cover all the aspects of various personal computer configurations and disk operating systems, nor is it a complete primer on LOTUS 1-2-3. For those readers interested in learning more details about using LOTUS-based software, we recommend that you consult with the appropriate publications from the Lotus Development Corporation or West Publishing Company.

LOTUS 1-2-3, Verson 2.01 or higher is required to run the templates. For those not having access to LOTUS 1-2-3, these templates will also run with VPPlanner, Release 2. West has a student version of VPPlanner, Release 2 and a manual available for sale to students at a nominal cost.

HARDWARE AND SOFTWARE REQUIREMENTS:

An IBM PC or PC-compatible computer with two floppy disk drives and at least 256K of RAM (random access memory) is recommended at the minimum. The templates also can be used on a PC with LOTUS installed on hard disk drive.

RUNNING THE TEMPLATES

First, "boot" the computer using a DOS system disk. Take the DOS disk out of drive A: and replace it with the LOTUS system disk. Place the template diskette into drive B:. Enter the word "LOTUS" without the quotes after the A> prompt and press the return key. LOTUS will load. If the default disk drive contains the template diskette, LOTUS will automatically run the AUTO123 file and you may begin using the templates.

If LOTUS does not default to the disk drive in which the template diskette is located, use the File Directory Command to change the default disk drive and then use the File Retrieve Command to load the AUTO123 file.

Note to hard disk users: The commands necessary to run LOTUS depend upon the user configuration of the hard disk. Please consult with your professor or computer consultant for help if you are unable to begin.

After invoking the AUTO123 file, the opening menu will appear as follows:

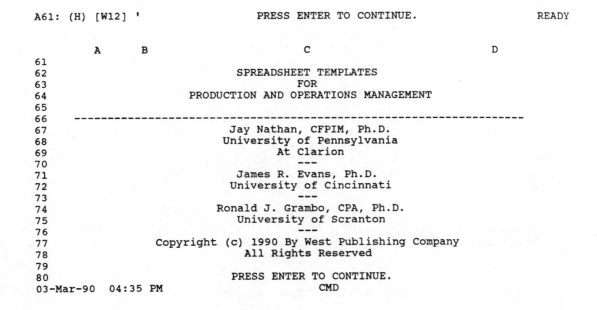

A61: (H) [W12] '   PRESS ENTER TO CONTINUE.   READY

```
          A      B                 C                      D
61
62                         SPREADSHEET TEMPLATES
63                                FOR
64                 PRODUCTION AND OPERATIONS MANAGEMENT
65
66        ------------------------------------------------------------
67                         Jay Nathan, CFPIM, Ph.D.
68                         University of Pennsylvania
69                                At Clarion
70                                  ---
71                         James R. Evans, Ph.D.
72                         University of Cincinnati
73                                  ---
74                     Ronald J. Grambo, CPA, Ph.D.
75                         University of Scranton
76                                  ---
77                 Copyright (c) 1990 By West Publishing Company
78                         All Rights Reserved
79
80                         PRESS ENTER TO CONTINUE.
03-Mar-90   04:35 PM              CMD
```

At this point just press the return key, and the MAIN MENU will appear as follows:

```
A1: [W12]                                                          READY


         A        B                    C                      D
  1                         M A I N    M E N U
  2
  3              Highlight the item of your choice and press ENTER.
  4
  5                  MOVING AVERAGE
  6                  EXPONENTIAL SMOOTHING
  7                  FACILITY LOCATION   (Scoring Model)
  8                  FACILITY LOCATION   (Gravity Model)
  9                  WORK MEASUREMENT (Standard Time)
 10                  ECONOMIC ORDER QUANTITY (EOQ)
 11                  ECONOMIC LOT SIZE (ELS)
 12                  AGGREGATE PLANNING
 13                  MATERIALS REQUIREMENT PLANNING (MRP)
 14                  OPERATIONS SCHEDULING
 15                  CONTROL CHART FOR VARIABLES
 16                  CONTROL CHART FOR ATTRIBUTES
 17                  Quit Lotus and return to the operating system.
 18
 19
 20
23-Feb-90   10:23 AM                                          CAPS
```

Using UP or DOWN ARROW keys, select the desired template by highlighting the appropriate menu item and pressing the ENTER key. From this point on, instructions apply to this particular book and template package only. They are not to be understood as standard commands in LOTUS or other electronic spreadsheets. Each of the following chapters provide information on how to use the various templates and solve production and operations management problems.

ABOUT LOTUS 1-2-3 AND THE TEMPLATE PACKAGE

LOTUS 1-2-3 is a software package that allows the user to perform three basic applications on a computer: spreadsheet analysis, graphics, and database management. A spreadsheet is a matrix of rows and columns. The intersection of each row with each column is called a <u>cell</u>. Each cell can hold data in the form of numbers or words. Examples of spreadsheets include a balance sheet, a gradebook, a schedule, and a budget. An electronic spreadsheet is a spreadsheet that exists electronically on a computer. One of the advantages of using an electronic spreadsheet is that all calculations are performed automatically. All you have to do is type in the numbers and formulas for the calculations and the answers to the computations are automatically calculated. The inputs can be changed or modified to perform "what if" analyses of various decision alternatives. Thus, the user of the templates can see the results for various scenarios and choose the best decision relevant to a particular situation.

The templates in this package are electronic spreadsheets that have package-defined output areas and user-defined input areas. A template has two types of cells. The first type consists of the cells in which data are entered, and the second type consists of the cells which have formulas entered in them. In this package, the templates are electronic spreadsheets into which the formulas for the calculations have already been entered. The user simply needs only to type in the numbers for a particular problem, the results are provided by the templates automatically.

The rest of this chapter covers the basic spreadsheet

operations that are needed in order to solve production and opertions management problems with this package. It would probably be best for newcomers to electronic spreadsheets to read this chapter at least once.

CHOOSING AN OPTION FROM A MENU:

A menu is a point in the LOTUS program which allows the choice from one of several options. If the word MENU is in the upper right-hand corner and CMD is on bottom line of the computer screen, the user is said to be in the menu-mode. When in menu-mode, you can choose one of the options which are listed on the second line of the screen.

In LOTUS, there are two ways to choose an option. The first way is simply to type the first letter of the option desired. Another way to choose an option is to highlight that option by using the right and left arrow keys. When the desired option is highlighted, press the return key.

MOVING THE CURSOR IN A SPREADSHEET

To enter data in a template, you must first learn how to move the cursor. The cursor is an indicator of the position on the screen where data typed from the keyboard will be placed on the screen. The cursor in a LOTUS spreadsheet on our templates is a highlighted rectangular block. The easiest way to move the cursor is to use the four arrow keys. The UP arrow will cause the cursor to move one row up, the DOWN arrow one row down, etc.

ENTERING DATA INTO A CELL

Move the cursor over the cell in which you wish to enter data. Type the numbers or words that are to be entered into that cell. The keys that you press are shown on the second line of the screen. When typing is finished, press the return key. The data typed can now be seen in the cell.

LOTUS classifies data into two types - values and labels. The type of data in a particular cell is important to LOTUS. The program treats one type of data differently from the other in many of the program's procedures. For our purposes, values can be considered as numbers, and labels can be considered as words. When you start typing data into a cell, LOTUS determines whether the data is a value or a label by the first character that is typed. After that first character, LOTUS is assuming a data type and allows the user to enter only certain characters. For example, suppose you wish to type "1ST QUARTER" into a cell. The first character you enter will be 1. Since this is a number, LOTUS assumes that the cell entry is going to be a value (a number) as indicated by the VALUE on the first line on the screen. LOTUS will be confused when the ENTER key is pressed because it sees "S" which is not a number as the second character. You will be placed in the EDIT mode as indicated on the first line of the screen. The EDIT mode can be cleared by pressing the ESC key twice. One way to indicate to LOTUS that this data is a label and not a number is to type a ^ (caret) before the 1. The ^ is called a label-prefix, and will not be shown in the cell.

CHANGING DATA IN A CELL

To change data in a cell, move the cursor to the cell (using arrow keys) containing the data which you wish to change. Enter the new data and press the ENTER key. This will replace the old data in that cell.

CORRECTING AN ERROR

Any time the word ERROR is shown in the upper right-hand corner of the screen, you have done something to place LOTUS in error mode. To clear the error mode, press the ESC key. The most common error with these templates is trying to enter data into a protected cell. Protected cells are those which you are not allowed to tamper with, or you might ruin the calculations that must be made. For other errors, consult a LOTUS text or your instructor. If you get stuck and don't know what to do, one of the alternatives is to reboot the computer and start over. However, this will cause all data that you have entered (after the last save) into the template to be erased. You will have to re-enter data from the beginning.

MENU OPTIONS IN ALL TEMPLATES

The primary menu in each template contains PRINT, SAVE, MAIN, CLEAN, and QUIT. The PRINT option allows you to print a copy of the spreadsheet. Be sure that your printer is turned on before selecting this option.

Unless the SAVE command is used, any data that has been changed will be lost when you leave the template. Each program template has a SAVE option that can be used after completing a problem. When saving a template, you should use a descriptive name for easy recall later. For example, MAPROB2 might stand for Moving Average, Problem 2. You may enter up to 8 characters in a name. These 8 characters should be letters or digits only. Do <u>not</u> use a period or extension when naming a file in LOTUS. If there has been a previously-saved file under the name being used now, LOTUS will ask you if you wish to Cancel or Replace. Press C (for Cancel) or simply hit the ENTER key while the Cancel is highlighted, the file will not be saved. Typing R to this query will cause the file previously stored under that name to be removed from the disk and replaced with the current template (file) name.

If you select MAIN, you will return to the main opening menu and <u>any data you entered will be lost unless you have saved it.</u> The CLEAN option will erase any data you have entered in the spreadsheet and allow you to start over. This is useful if you want to begin a new problem using the same template. Finally, the QUIT option will allow you to exit from the template package.

RETRIEVING DATA THAT HAVE BEEN PREVIOUSLY SAVED

Previously-saved LOTUS files can be retrieved from LOTUS by using a "File Retrieve" command. First make sure that the word READY is in the upper right-hand corner of the screen by pressing the ESC key a few times. Then type: forward slash (/), f, and r. LOTUS will now ask you for the name of the file to be retrieved. Type in the name and press ENTER key.

PRINTING A GRAPH

The first step in obtaining a printout of a graph is to have the template with the graph on the screen. Make sure that READY is shown in the upper right-hand corner of the screen by pressing ESC key a few times. Now, enter the Graph Save command by pressing: forward slash (/), g, and s. LOTUS will then ask you for the name of the file in which to save the graph. Enter up to 8 characters and press return. Please read SAVING DATA ENTERED INTO A TEMPLATE for the general rules of saving files using LOTUS. Also, note that the Graph Save command saves a picture of the graph. It does not save the template data file. So if you desire to keep the data that have been put into the template, you must save the entire file.

To obtain the actual graph printout, you must use the LOTUS PrintGraph program. To do this, you must return to the LOTUS Access System Menu and call the PrintGraph program. From the READY mode (press Esc a few times), enter these keystrokes: forward slash (/), q, and y. You will now be in the LOTUS

Access System menu. Choose the PrintGraph Option and LOTUS will ask you to replace the diskette in drive A with the PrintGraph disk. (Hard-disk users will not have to replace disks.) The PrintGraph menu on the screen will automatically have the IMAGE-SELECT option highlighted. Choose this option. On the screen, you should now see the name of the file in which you saved the graph. Highlight the name of the graph to be printed and press the space bar. This will put a # in front of the name. Press the return key to get back to the main PrintGraph menu. Now choose the Go option. Your graph will be generated and printed. When the WAIT in the upper right-hand corner of the screen stop flashing and MENU appears, choose the EXIT option from the menu to return to the LOTUS Access System. To return to the spread-sheet part of LOTUS, choose the 1-2-3 option from the LOTUS Access System menu.

Chapter 2
MOVING AVERAGE

Introduction

The method of moving averages attempts to smooth out the irregular components of a time series. The moving average associated with any time period is simply an average of the most recent n data values in the time series. The term "moving" average is based on the fact that as a new observation becomes available for the time series, the new observation replaces the oldest observation and a new average is computed.

Using the Moving Average Template

To illustrate the use of the moving average template, we will use the Forecasting With Moving Averages example on page 97 of Chapter 3. The weekly sales of gasoline is shown in the table below. We will compute forecasts based on a 3-week moving average.

Week	Sales (1000s of gallons)	Week	Sales (1000s of gallons)
1	17	7	20
2	21	8	18
3	19	9	22
4	23	10	20
5	18	11	15
6	16	12	22

After you have invoked the moving average template from the main menu, the following screen will appear:

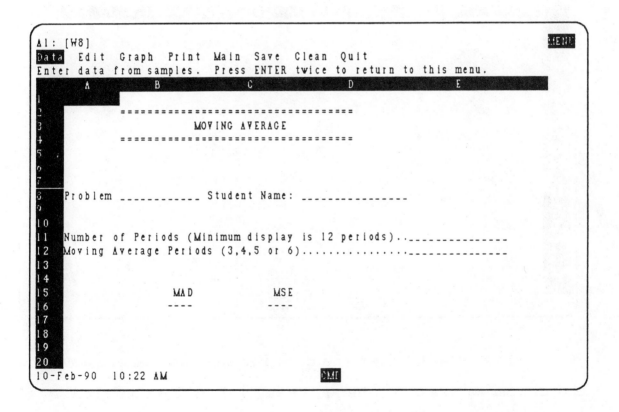

To begin, select DATA followed by NEW DATA. The template will prompt you for input regarding the problem name, your name, number of periods for the data, and the number of periods on which to base the moving average.   Use the ENTER key after inputting each response.   For this example, the number of periods of data is 12, and the number of periods for the moving average is 3.

The template will automatically create the necessary data input range and position the cursor to the cell for the first observation in the next screen.

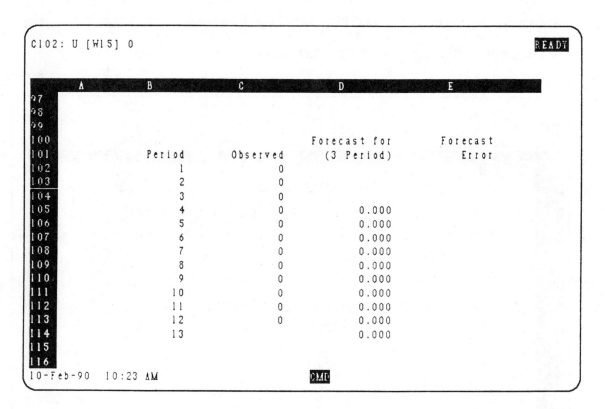

In this screen, enter the data for each period and move down the column by means of the ARROW key. Your results should look like the screen below (similar to Table 3.9 on page 99):

Period	Observation	Forecast for (3 period)	Forecast Error
1	17		
2	21		
3	19		
4	23	19	4.00
5	18	21	-3.00
6	16	20	-4.00
7	20	19	1.00
8	18	18	0.00
9	22	18	4.00
10	20	20	0.00
11	15	20	-5.00
12	22	19	3.00
13		19	

After all the data are entered, press the ENTER key. The template will return to the opening screen showing the calculated values of MAD and MSE.

Additional Options

1. From the main menu DATA option, you may select EXTEND DATA. This allows you to add additional observations to an existing time series.

2. From the main menu DATA option, you may select PERIODS, which allows you to change the number of moving average periods on which to base your forecasts.

3. To view a graph of the time series and moving average forecasts (Figure 3.12), select the GRAPH option from the menu. An example graph is shown below.

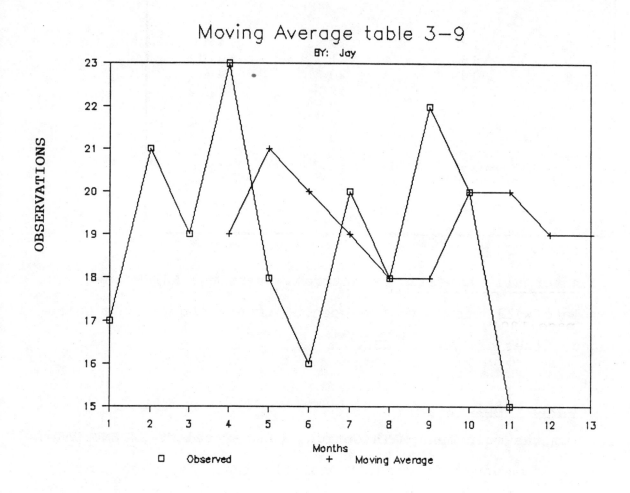

Moving Average table 3-9

BY: Jay

TEXT EXERCISES

1. Suppose that the quarterly sales values for the seven years of historical data are as follows:

	QTR 1	QTR 2	QTR 3	QTR 4	TOTAL SALES
Year 1	6	15	10	4	35
Year 2	10	18	15	7	50
Year 3	14	26	23	12	75
Year 4	19	28	25	18	90
Year 5	22	34	28	21	105
Year 6	24	36	30	20	110
Year 7	28	40	35	27	130

Show the four-quarter moving average values for this time series. Plot both the original time series and the moving average series on the same graph. (Chapter 3, problem 9, page 120).

2. Refer to the gasoline sales time series data in the example above.

a. Compute 4- and 5-week moving averages for the time series.

b. Compute the mean square error (MSE) for the 4- and 5-week moving average forecasts.

c. What appears to be the best number of weeks of past data to use in the moving average computation? Remember that the MSE for the 3-week moving average is 10.22. (Chapter 3, problem 13, page 121).

3. The Costello Music Company has been in business five years. The quarterly sales data are shown below.

	QTR 1	QTR 2	QTR 3	QTR 4	Total yearly Sales
Year 1	4	2	1	5	12
Year 2	6	4	4	14	28
Year 3	10	3	5	16	34
Year 4	12	9	7	22	50
Year 5	18	10	13	35	76

Show the four-quarter moving average values for this time series. Plot both the original time series and the moving average series on the same graph.

4. Case Problem

The Vintage Restaurant is located on Captive Island, a resort community near Fort Meyers, Florida. The restaurant, which is owned and operated by Karen Payne, has just completed its third year of operation. During this period of time Karen has sought to establish a reputation for the restaurant as a high-quality dining establishment that specializes in fresh seafood. The efforts made by Karen and her staff have proved successful, and her restaurant has become one of the best and fastest-growing restaurants on the island. Karen has concluded that in order to plan better for the growth of the restaurant in the future, it is necessary to develop a

system that will enable her to forecast food and beverage

sales by month for up to 1 year in advance.   Karen has available data on the total food and beverage sales that were realized during the previous 3 years of operation. These data are provided below.

Month	First Year	Second Year	Third Year
January	242	263	282
February	235	238	255
March	232	247	265
April	178	193	205
May	184	193	210
June	140	149	160
July	145	157	166
August	152	161	174
September	110	122	126
October	130	130	148
November	152	167	173
December	206	230	235

Perform an analysis of the sales data for the Vintage Restaurant. Prepare a report for Karen that summarizes your findings, forecasts, and recommendations. Include information on the following:

a.   A graph of the time series.

b.   Compute 4- and 5- month moving averages for the time series.

c.   Compute the mean square error (MSE) and mean absolute deviation (MAD) for the 4- and 5-month moving average forecasts.

SUPPLEMENTARY EXERCISES

1. The quarterly sales data for a college textbook over the
    past 3 years are as follows:

	Year 1	Year 2	Year 3
Quarter 1	1690	1800	1850
Quarter 2	940	900	1100
Quarter 3	2625	2900	2930
Quarter 4	2500	2360	2615

    Show the four-quarter moving average values for this time
    series.   Plot both the original time series and the moving
    averages on the same graph.

2. The following table represents three years of expenses for
    a six-unit apartment house in Southern Florida.

Month	Year 1	Year 2	Year 3
January	170	180	195
February	180	205	210
March	205	215	230
April	230	245	280
May	240	265	290
June	315	330	390
July	360	400	420
August	290	335	330
September	240	260	290
October	240	270	295
November	230	255	280
December	195	220	250

    a. Show 4 and 5 month moving average forecasts.

    b. Which one provides the best forecast?   Explain your
    reasoning.

3. Sales of industrial robots at MARKAL Robotics over the past

12 months are shown below.

Month	Sales (thousands)
January	22
February	20
March	19
April	21
May	23
June	18
July	25
August	17
September	21
October	18
November	23
December	19

a. Using 3 and 4 month moving average, determine the forecasts for industrial robots for the next month.

b. Evaluate the forecasting accuracies of the 3 and 4 month moving average results from part (a) using MAD and MSE measures.

Chapter 3
EXPONENTIAL SMOOTHING

Introduction

    Exponential smoothing is a forecasting technique that uses a weighted average of past time series values in order to forecast the value of the time series in the next period. The basic exponential smoothing model is

$$F_{t+1} = \alpha Y_t + (1 - \alpha)F_t$$

where

F_{t+1} = forecast of the time series for period t + 1

Y_t = actual value of the time series in period t

F_t = forecast of the time series for period t

α = smoothing constant ($0 <= \alpha <= 1$)

Exponential smoothing is discussed in Section 3.7 of the text.

Using the Exponential Smoothing Template

To illustrate the use of the template, we will use the gasoline sales time series in the Forecasting With Exponential Smoothing example on page 101 of Chapter 3. The table below shows twelve periods of sales data.

Week	Sales (1000s of gallons)	Week	Sales (1000s of gallons)
1	17	7	20
2	21	8	18
3	19	9	22
4	23	10	20
5	18	11	15
6	16	12	22

After you have invoked the exponential smoothing template from the main menu, the following screen will appear:

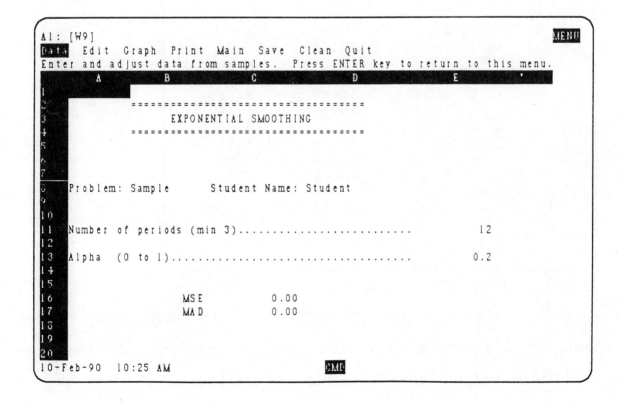

To begin, select DATA followed by NEW DATA. The template will prompt you for input regarding the problem name (GASOLINE), your name, number of periods of data (12), and the value of alpha (0.2). Use the ENTER key after inputting each response. (The number of periods must at least be three, and the alpha value must be between 0 and 1.) The template will automatically create the necessary data input range.

In the next screen, enter the data for each period by moving down the column by means of ARROW key. Your results should look like the screen below (similar to Table 3.10).

Period	Actual Observation	Forecast	Forecast Error
1	17		
2	21	17.00	4.00
3	19	17.80	1.20
4	23	18.04	4.96
5	18	19.03	-1.03
6	16	18.83	-2.83
7	20	18.26	1.74
8	18	18.61	-0.61
9	22	18.49	3.51
10	20	19.19	0.81
11	15	19.35	-4.35
12	22	18.48	3.52
13		19.18	

After all data are entered, press the ENTER key. The template will return to the opening screen, showing the calculated values of MSE and MAD, as shown below.

```
-------------------------------------------
          EXPONENTIAL     SMOOTHING
-------------------------------------------


Problem  Text Example      Student Name _____

Number of Periods (minimum 3)  12_____

Alpha (0 to 1)  .2_____


          MSE     8.98

          MAD     2.60
```

Additional Options

1. From the main menu DATA option, you may select EXTEND DATA. This allows you to add additional observations to an existing time series.

2. From the main menu EDIT option, you may select EDIT, which returns you to the data screen and allows you to change the values of the observations.

3. From the main menu EDIT option, you may select ALPHA, which allows you to change the value of the smoothing constant in the opening data input screen.

4. To view a graph of the time series and forecasts (Figure

3.13), select the GRAPH option from the menu. An example graph
is shown below.

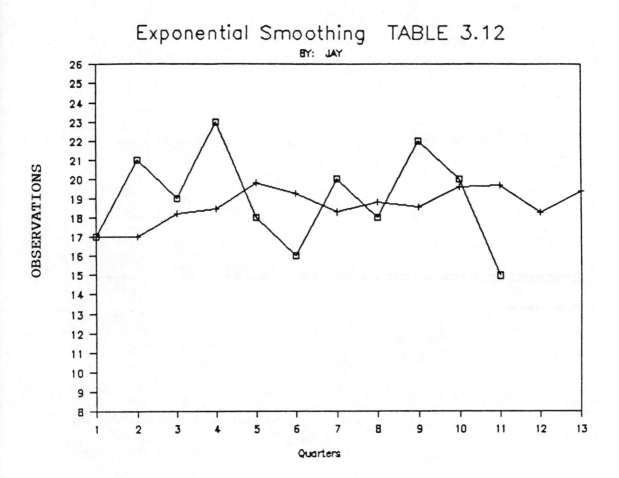

TEXT EXERCISES

1. The following time series shows the sales of a particular
    product over the past 12 months:

Month	1	2	3	4	5	6
Sales	105	135	120	105	90	120

Month	7	8	9	10	11	12
Sales	145	140	100	80	100	110

    Use Alpha = 0.3 to compute the exponential smoothing values
    for the time series. (Chapter 3, problem 19, page 122).

2. Analyze the forecasting errors for the time series in
    problem 1 by using a smoothing constant of 0.5.   Does a
    smoothing constant of 0.3 or 0.5 appear to provide the
    better forecasts? (Chapter 3, problem 20, page 122).

3. The number of component parts used in a production
    process each week in the last 10 weeks showed the
    following:

Week	Parts	Week	Parts
1	200	6	210
2	350	7	280
3	250	8	350
4	360	9	290
5	250	10	320

    Use a smoothing constant of 0.25 to develop the exponential
    smoothing values for this time series.   Indicate your

forecast for next week. (Chapter 3, problem 21, page 122).

4. A chain of grocery stores experienced the following weekly demand (cases) for a particular brand of automatic dishwasher detergent:

Week	1	2	3	4	5	6	7	8	9	10
Demand	22	18	23	21	17	24	20	19	18	21

Use exponential smoothing with Alpha = 0.2 in order to develop a forecast for week 11. (Chapter 3, problem 22, page 122).

5. United Dairies, Inc. supplies milk to several independent grocers throughout Dade County in Florida. Management of United Dairies would like to develop a forecast of the number of half-gallons of milk sold per week. Sales data for the past 12 weeks are as follows:

Week	1	2	3	4	5	6
Sales (units)	2750	3100	3250	2800	2900	3050

Week	7	8	9	10	11	12
Sales (units)	3300	3100	2950	3000	3200	3150

Use the above 12 weeks of data and exponential smoothing with Alpha = 0.4 to develop a forecast of demand for the 13th week. (Chapter 3, problem 23, page 123).

6. Use the gasoline sales data and exponential smoothing
    forecasts for Alpha = 0.3

    a.   Compute the mean absolute deviation (MAD) measure of
    forecast accuracy.

    b.   The exponential smoothing forecasts for alpha = 0.2 and
    alpha = 0.3 provided the following MSE measures of forecast
    accuracy:

Alpha	MSE
0.2	8.98
0.3	9.35

    The MAD measure for Alpha = 0.2 is 2.596. Using the results
    of part(a) above, does the MAD criterion also support the
    use of Alpha = 0.2 as the better smoothing constant.

SUPPLEMENTARY EXERCISES

1.   The following table represents monthly sales data for a name
     brand watches in a department store.

Month	Sales
1	100
2	105
3	98
4	95
5	120
6	115
7	104
8	85
9	112
10	130
11	135
12	145

a. Use single exponential smoothing to forecast demand using alpha = 0.1.

b. Use single exponential smoothing to forecast demand using alpha = 0.2.

c. Based on MSE and MAD forecast accuracy criteria, would you prefer a smoothing coefficient of 0.1 or 0.2 ?

2. Sales for PAPA GINO's Pizza for the past seven months are shown below.

January	195
February	152
March	120
April	115
May	100
June	110
July	119

a. For alpha = 0.3, forecast August sales using the exponential smoothing forecasting model.

b. If you are allowed to use smoothing coefficients of 0.3, 0.4, and 0.5, which one would you choose based on the mean absolute deviation (MAD) forecast accuracy measure?

3. MARKAL industries have been testing with a new product. The following table shows the product's first nine months sales.

January	95
February	125
March	160
April	175
May	165
June	165
July	155
August	150
September	155

a. Use exponential smoothing to forecast sales from April through September. Select alpha = 0.6.

b. Repeat part (a) with an alpha of 0.2.

c. Repeat part (a) using a three-month moving average.

d. Which forecasting method should be used for the October forecast? Explain.

Chapter 4
FACILITY LOCATION (Scoring Model)

Introduction

    Scoring models are often used in facility location studies to rate alternative sites. Each major location criterion is broken down into several levels. A score is assigned to each level that reflects the relative importance of that criterion. The site having the highest score is the best candidate for more detailed consideration. The use of scoring models for facility location is discussed in Section 7.2 of the text.

Using the Scoring Model Template

    To illustrate the use of this template we will use the Halvorsen Supply Company example found in Chapter 7, page 264 of the text. The Halvorsen Supply Company has identified two sites for a new facility. The company has identified the following six (6) criteria:

1. Climate
2. Water availability
3. Schools
4. Housing
5. Community attitude
6. Labor laws

Climate, Water Availability, Schools, and Housing each have six levels, ranging from 0 to 5; while Community Attitude and Labor Laws have five levels, ranging from 0 to 4. The following weights are assigned to each of these criteria.

```
Climate              ...  6
Water availability   ...  2
Schools              ...  4
Housing              ...  2
Community attitude   ... 15
Labor laws           ...  8
```

The Halvorsen Supply Company management has evaluated two sites, A and B, as follows.

Criteria	Site A	Site B
Climate	3	5
Water	4	3
Schools	3	2
Housing	5	3
Community	3	3
Labor laws	2	3

After invoking the scoring model template from the main menu, the following screen will be displayed:

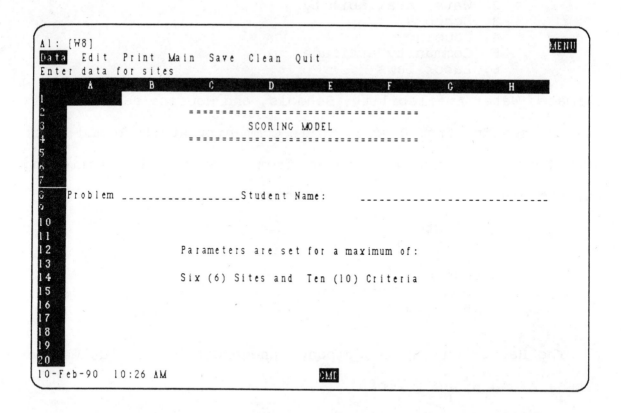

To begin, select DATA from the menu and you will be asked to provide a problem name and your name. After pressing the ENTER key following you name, the template then displays the data screen shown below.

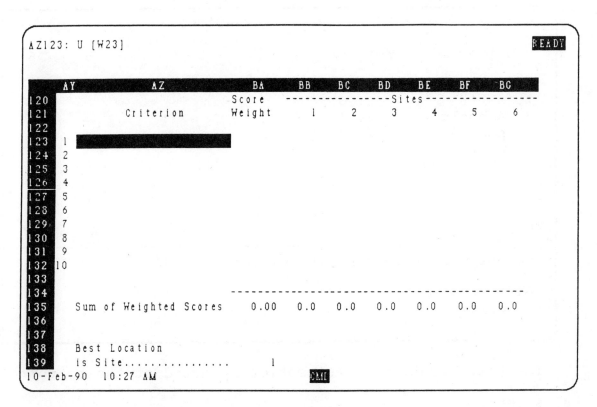

Use the ARROW keys to move about the screen, inputting in
the name of each criterion, its weight, and the scores for each
site. The resuts are shown below.

```
                    Score ------------Sites-----------------

        Criterion   Weight    1     2     3     4     5     6

    1.  climate      6.00     3     5
    2.  water        2.00     4     3
    3.  schools      4.00     3     2
    4.  housing      2.00     5     3
    5.  community   15.00     3     3
    6.  labor laws   8.00     2     3
    7.
    8.
    9.
   10.
                    ---------------------------------------------
    Sum of weighted scores 109.0 119.0

    Best location
    is Site..........2
```

The best location is automatically noted at the bottom of the screen.

Additional Options

1. From the main menu, you may select EDIT and revise any values or add sites or criteria up to the maximum limits.

TEXT EXERCISES

1. An industrialist faced with the choice among four possible locations uses a scoring model as shown below. Which location would be the best?

```
-------------------------------------------------
                                    Location
Criteria          Weight    1      2      3      4
-------------------------------------------------
Raw material
  availability      0.2      G      P      OK     VG

Infrastructure     0.1      OK     OK     OK     OK

Transportation     0.5      VG     OK     P      OK
  costs

Labor relations    0.1      G      VG     P      OK

Quality of life    0.1      G      VG     P      OK

        Points   VG = very good : 5 points
                  G = good       : 4 points
                 OK = acceptable: 3 points
                  P = poor       : 1 point
-------------------------------------------------
```

(Problem 1, Chapter 7, page 282)

2. Goslin Chemicals has decided to build a new plant in the sunbelt in order to take advantage of new solar-powered heating units used in chemical production. Three sites have been proposed: Phoenix, Arizona; El Paso, Texas; and Mountain Home, Arkansas.

a. Construct a scoring model using the criteria and their weights indicated in the example illustrated for the use of the template.

1. climate
2. water
3. labor
4. attitude
5. schools
6. housing

b. Suppose the three sites have ratings given below. Under the system constructed in (a), which seems to be more preferable?

Factor	Level Assigned		
	Phoenix	El Paso	Mountain Home
Climate	5	5	4
Water	3	5	5
Labor	1	2	4
Attitude	3	3	4
Schools	5	3	2
Housing	4	2	3

(Problem 2, Chapter 7, page 282).

SUPPLEMENTARY EXERCISES

1. MARKAL manufacturing company is looking to build a new facility for their line of educational products. Three locations have been suggested: Princeton, New Jersey; White Plains, New York; and Scranton, Pennsylvania.

a. Construct a scoring model using the following criteria in which the factors have these priorities:

1.   competition   20%

2.   labor unions   10%

3.   favorable tax   20%

4.   quality supplier   15%

5.   local politics   5%

6.   market proximity   30%

Top management has assigned the following points to the three locations:

Level Assigned

Factor	Princeton	White Plains	Scranton
competition	30	18	9
labor union	8	13	10
favorable tax	12	22	13
quality supplier	25	20	8
local politics	38	23	19
market proximity	40	31	5

2.   Suppose the three locations have the ratings given below. Under the system constructed in (a), which seems to be most preferred?

Level Assigned

Factor	Princeton	White Plains	Scranton
competition	5	4	5
labor union	1	3	2
favorable tax	3	2	3
quality supplier	4	5	3
local politics	1	2	4
market proximity	4	5	1

Chapter 5
FACILITY LOCATION (Gravity Model)

<u>Introduction</u>

The center of gravity method is an analytical technique for determining the location of a central facility such as a warehouse, based primarily on cost considerations. The method takes into account the locations of plants and markets, the volume of goods moved, and the transportation costs in arriving at a best location for a single intermediate warehouse. The <u>center of gravity</u> is the location that minimizes the weighted distance between the warehouse and its supply and distribution points, where the distance is weighted by the volume supplied or consumed. The center of gravity method is discussed in Section 7.4 of the text.

<u>Using the Center of Gravity Template</u>

To illustrate the use of this template we consider the

Taylor Paper Products example found in the Chapter 7, page 269. Taylor Paper Products is a producer of paper stock used in newspapers and magazines. Taylor's demand is relatively constant and can be forecast rather accurately. The company's two plants are located in Hamilton, Ohio, and Kingsport, Tennessee. These plants distribute paper stock to four major markets: Chicago, Pittsburgh, New York, and Atlanta. The board of directors has authorized the construction of an intermediate warehouse to service these customers. Coordinates for the plants and markets are shown below.

	X	Y
Hamilton	58	96
Kingsport	80	70
Chicago	30	120
Pittsburgh	90	110
New York	127	130
Atlanta	65	40

The table below indicates the capacities for various plants and markets.

	Location	Production/Usage (tons per months)
Plants	1. Hamilton	400
	2. Kingsport	300
Markets	3. Chicago	200
	4. Pittsburgh	100
	5. New York	300
	6. Atlanta	100

After invoking the center of gravity template, the following screen will be shown:

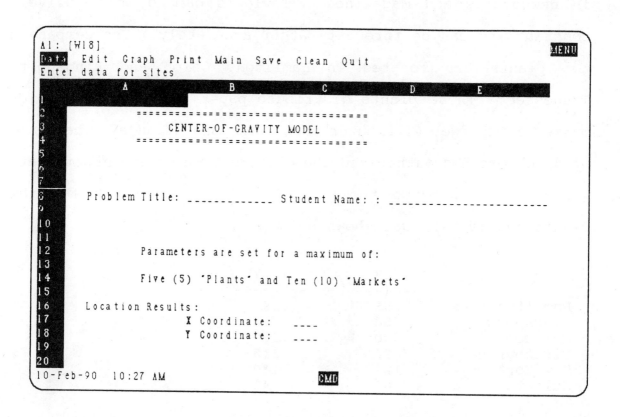

You will be prompted for the title of the problem and your name. After pressing the ENTER key, the data input screen will be displayed.

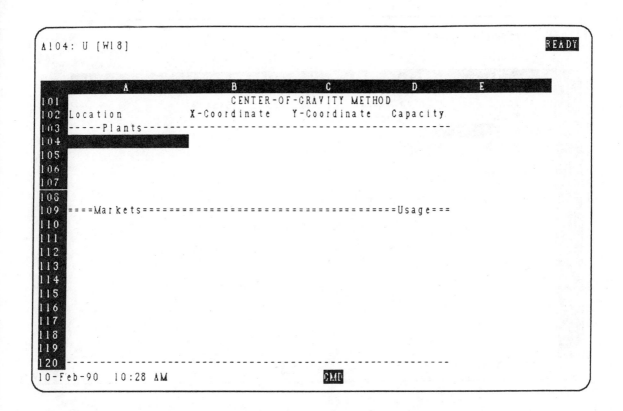

You are now ready to input coordinates and capacity values by using arrow keys. For example, type "Hamilton", use right ARROW key to move under X-coordinate and type 58; type in the Y-coordinate and so on, until you have entered all the plant and market names as well as the coordinates and capacities. The completed screen will look like the one below.

```
A104: U [Wl8] 'Hamilton                                         READ

              A              B              C              D         E
101                          CENTER-OF-GRAVITY METHOD
102  Location         X-Coordinate   Y-Coordinate   Capacity
103  -----Plants----------------------------------------------------
104  Hamilton                  58             96           400
105  Kingston                  80             70           300
106
107
108
109  ====Markets=======================================Usage===
110  Chi                       30            120           200
111  Pitts                     90            110           100
112  NY                       127            130           300
113  Atl                       65             40           100
114
115
116
117
118
119
120  -----------------------------------------------------
10-Feb-90   10:52 AM                      CMD
```

After you have completed the input, press ENTER key. You will return to the opening template screen. The coordinates for center-of-gravity will be shown at the bottom of the first screen.

Additional Options

1. From the main menu, you may select EDIT to change coordinates or capacities or to add or delete sites.

2. You may also select GRAPH, which displays a graph of the locations and the center of gravity on a coordinate system similar to Figure 7.6 in the text. An example is shown below.

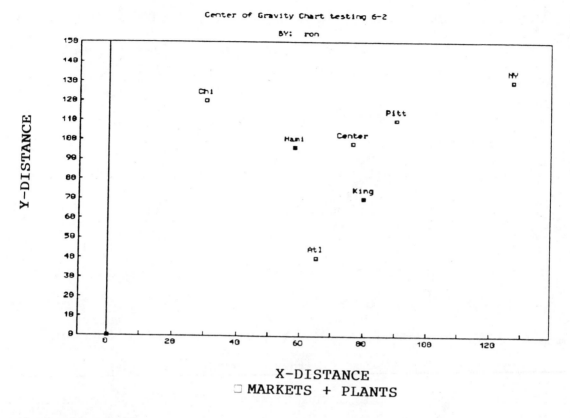

Center of Gravity Chart testing 6-2

BY: ron

TEXT EXERCISES

1. Given the following locational information and volume of
    material movements from a supply point to several retail
    outlets, find the optimal location for the supply point
    using the center of gravity method.

Retail Outlet	Location Coordinates x	Location Coordinates Y	Material Movements
1	20	5	1200
2	18	15	1800
3	3	16	1600
4	3	4	1100
5	16	20	2000

(Chapter 7, problem 3, page 283)

2. Broderick's Burgers would like to determine the best location for drawing customers from three population centers. The map coordinates of the three centers are given as follows:

Population center 1 $X1 = 2$, $Y1 = 8$

Population center 2 $X2 = 6$, $Y2 = 6$

Population center 3 $X3 = 1$, $Y3 = 1$

a. What location will minimize the total distance from the three centers?

b. Population center 1 is four times as large as center 3, and center 2 is twice as large as center 3. The firm feels that the importance of locating near a population center is proportional to its population. Find the best location under these assumptions. (Chapter 7, problem 4, page 283).

3. A large metropolitan campus needs to erect a parking garage for students, faculty, and visitors. The garage has a planned capacity of 1000 cars. Based on a survey, it is estimated that 30 percent of the arrivals to campus go to the business school and adjacent buildings; 40 percent go to the engineering complex; 20 percent to the University Center area, and 10 percent go to the administrative offices (see campus map in the text). Four potential sites (A, B, C, and D) are being considered. Which one would be best for the new garage? (Chapter 7, problem 5, page 284).

4. A national drug store chain prefers to operate one outlet in a town that has four major market segments. The number of potential customers in each segment along with the coordinates are given below.

Market Segment	Location Coordinates X	Coordinates Y	Number of Customers
1	2	18	1000
2	15	17	800
3	2	2	1500
4	14	2	2200

a. Which would be the best location using the center-of-gravity method?

b. If after five years, half the customers from segment 4 are expected to move to segment 2, where should the drug store shift, if the same criteria is adopted? (Chapter 7, problem 6, page 284).

SUPPLEMENTARY EXERCISES

1. Maxims Department Store has four locations throughout the city. Its parent corporation, J.C. Dollars, Inc. is investigating centralizing all distribution to these stores. Their plan calls for a central distribution center to accept all incoming merchandise, process the necessary paper work, and ship the goods to the individual stores. Since the

stores are of different sizes, the volume of merchandise differs. Maxims owns its own fleet of trucks for distribution. On a grid superimposed over the city, the four store locations and their monthly volumes are:

Store	X-coordinate	Y-coordinate	Volume (1000 pounds)
1	5	2	35
2	2	11	42
3	8	8	65
4	17	22	15

Determine the approximate location for the distribution center by finding the center of gravity.

2. MARKAL trucking company has three locations throughout the greater Pittsburg area. Recently, the management decided to establish a central order processing and service facility. Since the customer bases in three locations are different, the volume of orders and service needs differ considerably. MARKAL owns its own fleet of trucks for providing service to their customers. The following table provides the weekly orders for services:

Location	X-coordinate	Y-coordinate	Volume of orders
1	10	15	25
2	3	9	16
3	5	12	8

Determine the approximate location for the central order processing and service facility.

Chapter 6
WORK MEASUREMENT (Standard Time)

Introduction

The purpose of work measurement is to develop time standards for the performance of jobs. A time standard is defined as the amount of time it takes to perform a task by a trained operator working at a normal pace and using a prescribed method. Time study is a common technique for developing work standards. A time study is performed by observing the time to perform a work task over several cycles, rating the performance of the task, using the performance rating to determine the normal time, determining allowances for personal time, fatigue, and un-avoidable delays, and finally determining the standard time. Time study is discussed in Section 11.6 of the text.

Using the Work Measurement Template

To illustrate the use of the template, we will use the Freeland

Faucet example in Chapter 11 of the text. The template will
only allow you to develop standard times for an overall task or
for a single work element. Thus, for illustrative purposes, we
will use the cumulative times from Figure 11.13 on page 475.
These are given below.

```
        Observation   Time
        -----------   ----
             1         .51
             2         .53
             3         .58
             4         .56
             5         .54
             6         .49
             7         .54
             8         .55
             9         .62
            10         .52
            11         .55
```

We will assume that the performance rating is 1.0 for this task
and that the allowance percentage is 20%.

    After you have invoked the work measurement template from
the main menu, the following screen will appear:

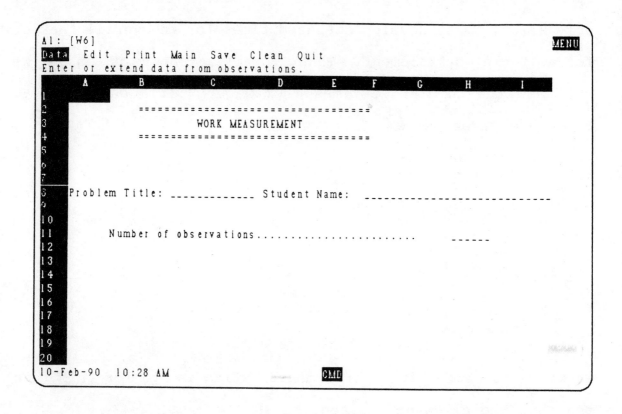

To begin, select DATA from the main menu. The template will prompt you for the problem title, your name, and the number of observations. Press the ENTER key after each response.

After completing this screen, the following screen will appear:

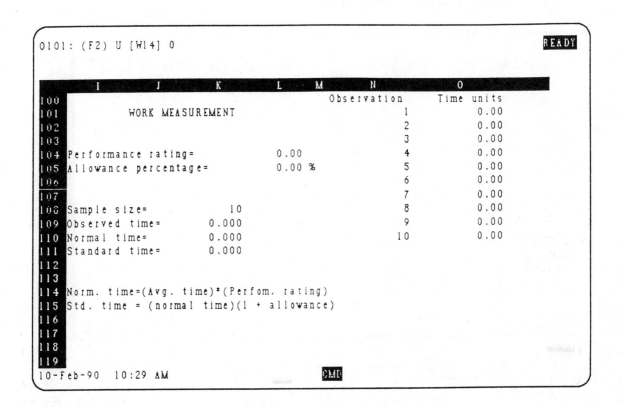

The cursor will be positioned for the first observation in the Time Units column. Use the down ARROW after entering each observation. After the last observation is entered, you will enter the performance rating (1.00) followed by the allowance percentage (20).

The results are shown below.

```
        WORK MEASUREMENT        Observation   Time units
                                    1            .51
                                    2            .53
                                    3            .58
    Performance rating =  1.0       4            .56
    Allowance percentage =  20%     5            .54
                                    6            .49
                                    7            .54
                                    8            .55
                                    9            .62
                                   10            .52
    Sample size        11          11            .55
    Observed time      .545
    Normal time        .545
    Standard time      .653
```

The reason that these results are different from the text is that the performance rating of each individual work element in the text example is not constant at 1.0. To handle this using the template, you would have to compute the standard time for each individual work element and add the resulting standard times.

Additional Options

1. You may select EDIT from the menu. This allows you to change any of the input data and recompute the standard time.

TEXT EXERCISES

1. Figure 11.15 (page 487) shows a partially completed time-
    study worksheet. Determine the standard time for this
    operation. Hint: use the template for each element and add
    the results. (Chapter 11, problem 15, page 486).

2. Compute the normal time for drilling a hole in a steel plate
    if the following observations (in minutes) have been
    observed. Use a rating factor of 1.00.

           .24   .25   .29   .24   .27

           .25   .245 .19   .20   .23

    (Chapter 11, problem 16, page 486)

3. Given the following time-study data conducted by continuous
    time measurement, compute the standard time. Use a fatigue
    allowance of 20 percent.

Activity	Cycle of Observations 1	2	3	4	5	Performance Rating
Get casting	0.21	2.31	4.41	6.45	8.59	0.95
Fix into fixture	0.48	2.59	4.66	6.70	8.86	0.90
Drilling operation	1.52	3.65	5.66	7.74	9.90	1.00
Unload	1.73	3.83	5.91	7.96	10.10	0.95
Inspect	1.98	4.09	6.15	8.21	10.30	0.80
Replace	2.10	4.20	6.25	8.34	10.42	1.10

Hint: Use the template for each activity and add the results for standard time. (Chapter 11, problem 17, page 486)

SUPPLEMENTARY EXERCISES

1.   Based on a time study, the following fifteen observations (in minutes) were recorded: 2.6, 2.8, 2.4, 2.7, 2.5, 3.1, 2.8, 2.9, 2.7, 2.8, 2.6, 2.4, 2.9, 2.6, and 2.6. The worker was performing at 95 percent efficiency, and the allowance is 30 percent. Determine the standard time (ST) for this job.

2.   Ten observations of a production operation (3.4, 3.6, 3.1, 3.9, 3.2, 3.8, 3.3, 3.7, 3.7, and 3.3) showed a mean time of 3.5 minutes. The worker was performing at 110 percent efficiency. The allowance factor is 25 percent. Determine the standard time (ST) for this job.

3.   In exercise 2, the first two observations were found to be erroneous; the correct values are 3.3 and 3.8. Compute the revised mean observed time and also determine the standard time for the job.   Use the same worker efficiency and allowance percentage.

4.   An apparel manufacturer's men's coat department had observed a worker in the pressing and inspection operations. Six observations were made, with performance ratings on each element. For each element, the various times are shown in the following table.

Element	Observation Times (seconds)						Performance Rating (percent)
	1	2	3	4	5	6	
Inspect front	7.6	7.3	8.2	7.8	8.0	8.1	105
Press front	15.0	15.9	16.0	17.0	16.1	17.0	110
Inspect lapel	5.0	6.0	7.0	6.1	6.3	8.0	100
Press lapel	20.0	18.0	19.0	18.5	20.0	18.0	105
Insp. lining	9.0	8.0	7.0	8.1	7.0	9.2	95
Hang up coat	4.0	3.9	5.0	6.0	6.0	5.1	115

Allowances are to be 20 percent. Determine the standard time (ST) for this job. Hint: For each element, use the template to get the standard time and then add them to get the standard time for the job.

Chapter 7
ECONOMIC ORDER QUANTITY (EOQ)

Introduction

The economic order quantity (EOQ) model is the most fundamental inventory model. It assumes that we seek an inventory policy for a single item under continuous review; the entire quantity arrives in inventory at one point in time; and the demand for the item has a constant rate. No stockouts are allowed. The EOQ model is discussed in Section 13.1 of the text.

Using the Economic Order Quantity Template

To illustrate the use of the template, we will use the Holton drug company example discussed in Section 13.1 of the text. The demand for one product, All-Bright toothpaste, has a constant demand rate of 2000 cases per month. Hence, the demand for 12 months can be approximated closely to 24000 cases. Holton estimates the annual inventory-holding costs to be 18 percent of the value of the inventory. Since the cost of one case of All-Bright toothpaste is $12.00, the cost of holding, or carrying one case of All-Bright in inventory for 1 year is .18($12.00) = $2.16. It costs Holton $38.00 to place an order, regardless of the quantity requested in the order. The company operates 250 working days per year, and the lead time is 3 days.

After you have invoked the economic order quantity template from the main menu, the following screen will appear:

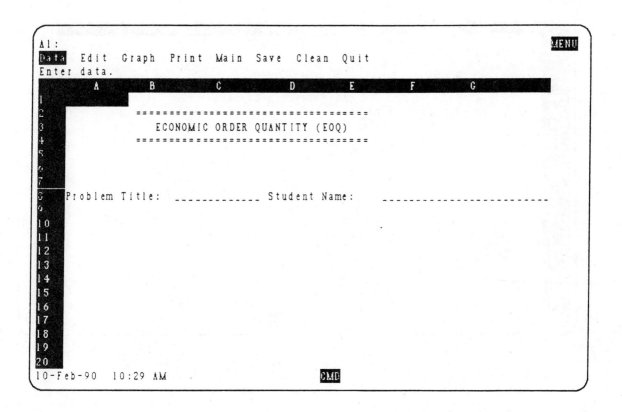

To begin, select DATA from the main menu. You will be prompted for the problem title and your name. Press ENTER after each response. The next screen will prompt you for the parameters of the problem. For the Holton Drug Company example, annual demand is 24,000; order cost in dollars is 38; carrying cost in dollars per year per unit is $2.16; number of operation days per year is 250; and lead time in days is 3. Use the ARROW key after each input.

The results are automatically calcuated as the inputs are entered:

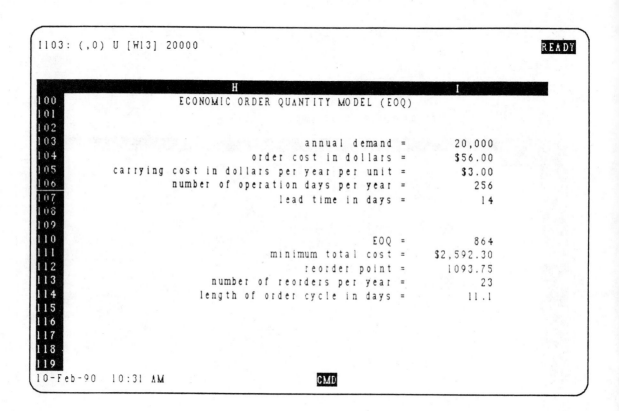

```
I103: (,0) U [W13] 20000                                        READY

                              H                               I
100              ECONOMIC ORDER QUANTITY MODEL (EOQ)
101
102
103                                 annual demand =        20,000
104                         order cost in dollars =        $56.00
105     carrying cost in dollars per year per unit =        $3.00
106            number of operation days per year =           256
107                          lead time in days =             14
108
109
110                                        EOQ =            864
111                         minimum total cost =       $2,592.30
112                              reorder point =        1093.75
113              number of reorders per year =              23
114            length of order cycle in days =            11.1
115
116
117
118
119
10-Feb-90  10:31 AM                    CMD
```

Pressing the ENTER key returns you to the starting screen and menu.

Additional Options

1. From the main menu, you may choose the EDIT option which allows you to change any of the input data and recompute the EOQ and cost.

2. You may also select GRAPH, which displays a graph of the relevant costs similar to Figure 13.3 on page 532 of the text. An example is shown below.

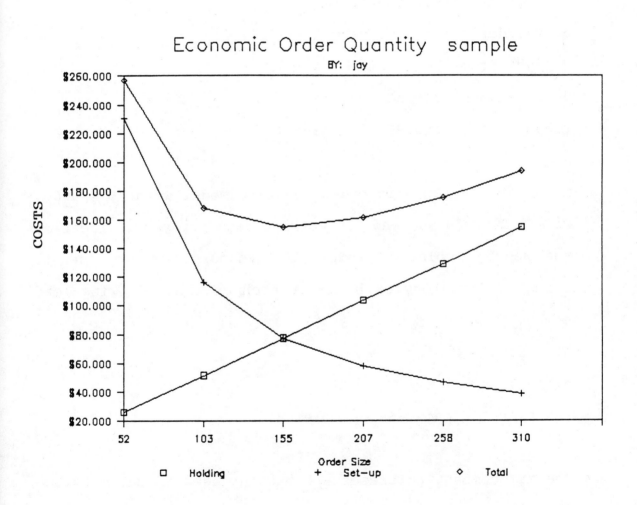

TEXT EXERCISES

1. Suppose that R&B Beverage Company has a soft-drink product that has a constant annual demand rate of 3600 cases. A case of the soft drink costs R&B $3. Ordering costs are $20 per order and inventory holding costs are charged at 25 percent of the cost per unit. There are 250 working days per year and the lead time is 5 days. Identify the following aspects of the inventory policy.

    a. economic order quantity

    b. reorder point

    c. cycle time

    d. total annual cost

    (Chapter 13, page 566, problem 1)

2. Consider the economic order quantity model with D = 5000, Co = $32, Ch = $2, and 250 working days per year. Identify the reorder point in terms of inventory position and in terms of inventory on hand for each of the following lead times:

    a. 5 days

    b. 15 days

    (Chapter 13, page 566, problem 3)

3. The XYZ company purchases a component used in the manufacture of automobile generators directly from the supplier. XYZ's generator production operation which is operated at

constant rate, will require 1000 components per month throughout the year. Assume ordering costs are $25 per order, unit cost is $2.50 per component, and annual inventory holding costs are charged at 20 percent. The company oerates 250 days per year and the lead time is 5 days.

a.   Compute the EOQ, total annual inventory holding and ordering costs, and the reorder point.

(Chapter 13, page 567, problem 4)

4.   Tele-Reco is a new specialty store that sells television sets, videotape recorders, video games, and other television-related products. A new Japanese manufactured videotape recorder costs Tele-Reco $600 per unit. Tele-Reco's inventory carrying cost is figured at an annual rate of 22 percent. Ordering costs are estimated to be $70 per order.

a.   If demand for the new videotape recorder is expected to be constant with a rate of 20 units per month, what is the recommended order quantity for the videotape recorder?

b.   What are the estimated annual inventory holding and ordering costs associated with this product?

c.   How many orders will be placed per year?

d.   With 250 working days per year, what is the cycle time for this product?

(Chapter 13, page 567, problem 5)

5. Cress Electronic Products manufactures components used in the automative industry. Cress purchases parts for use in its manufacturing operation from a variety of different suppliers. One particular supplier provides a part where the assumptions of the EOQ model are realistic. The annual demand is 5000 units. Ordering costs are $80 per order and inventory carrying costs are figured at an

   annual rate of 25 percent.

   a. If the cost of the part is $20 per unit, what is the economic order quantity?

   b. Assume 250 days of operation per year. If the lead time for an order is 12 days, what is the reorder point?

   c. If the lead time for the part is 7 weeks (35 days), what is the reorder point?

   (Chapter 13, page 568, problem 7)

SUPPLEMENTARY EXERCISES

1. Grethan Manufacturing Corporation uses 20,000 circuit boards each year in the production of personal computer systems. Order costs for the circuit boards is $50.00 and holding costs for one board is $1.50 per unit per year. What is the EOQ? What is the minimum total cost of inventory?

2. The MARKAL company produces brass greeting cards. The company expects next year's demand for greeting cards to be 20,000 at a uniform rate. The order cost is $100 and

holding costs are $2.00 per unit per year.   What is the economic order quantity? What is the reorder point? What is the minimum total cost of inventory?

3. The ABC company purchases electric motors used in the manufacturing of dryers. ABC's production operation, which is at a steady rate, requires 2000 motors per month throughout the year (24,000 units anually).   If ordering costs are $40.00 per order, unit cost is $3.00 per motor, and annual inventory holding costs are charged at 25%, provide answers to the following inventory policy questions for ABC.

a.   What is the EOQ for this electric motor?

b.   What are the total annual inventory holding and order-ing costs associated with your recommended EOQ?

c.   What is the length of cycle time in months?

4. Assuming 260 days of operation per year and a lead time of 5 days, what is the reorder point for the ABC company in exercise 3? What is the length of the order cycle in days?

Chapter 8
ECONOMIC LOT SIZE (ELS)

Introduction

The economic lot size (ELS) model assumes a constant supply rate over time, rather than inventory being replenished all at once as in the EOQ model. This model is designed for production situations in which once, an order is placed, production begins and a constant number of units are added to inventory each day until the production run has been completed. We also assume that the production rate is greater than the demand rate. This model is discussed in Section 13.3 of the text.

Using the Economic Lot Size Template

We shall illustrate the use of the ELS template with the Forum Shoes, Inc. example found in Chapter 13, page 540. Total annual demand for a particular shoe is 21,000 pairs. Forum's production costs are $22 per pair, with annual inventory holding cost figured at a 16 percent rate. The setup of the production line operation, including cleaning, preparation, and changeover from the previous production operation requires several hours of work, at a cost of $200. On an annual basis, the production capacity for the dress shoes is 50,000 pairs.

After you have invoked the economic lot size template from the main menu, the following screen will appear:

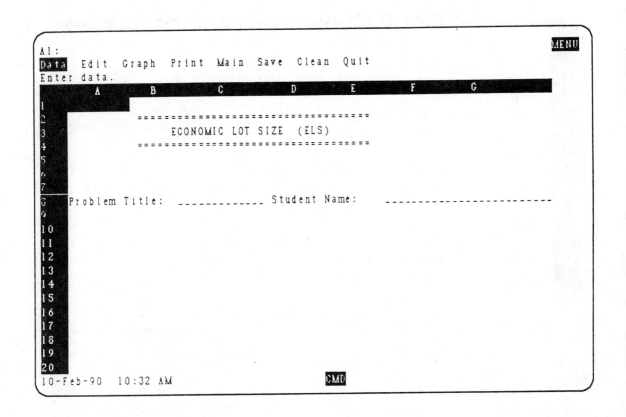

```
A1:                                                                    MENU
Data  Edit  Graph  Print  Main  Save  Clean  Quit
Enter data.
         A        B        C        D        E        F        G
1
2
3            ====================================
             ECONOMIC LOT SIZE  (ELS)
4            ====================================
5
6
7
8      Problem Title:  _____  Student Name:   _____
9
10
11
12
13
14
15
16
17
18
19
20
10-Feb-90  10:32 AM                            CMD
```

To begin, select DATA from the main menu. You will be prompted for the problem title and your name. Press the ENTER key after each response. The second screen will then appear and prompt you for the problem parameters just as in the EOQ template. For the example, annual demand is 21,000; setup cost is \$200; carrying cost per year per unit is \$3.52 (.16 X \$22); annual production capacity is 50,000; number of operating days per year is 250; and lead time is 5 days. Use the DOWN ARROW key after each input.

The input and the results are:

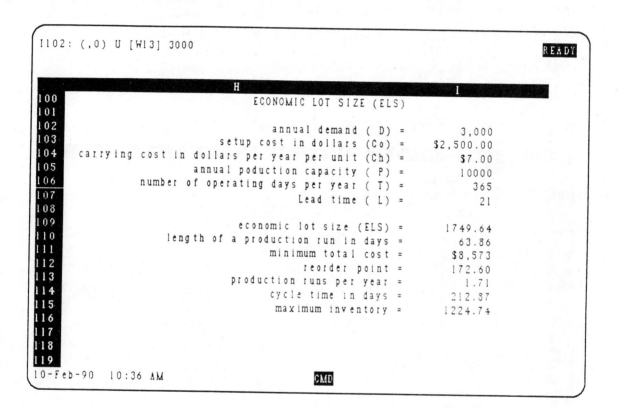

```
I102: (,0) U [W13] 3000                                              READY

                               H                              I
100                    ECONOMIC LOT SIZE (ELS)
101
102                           annual demand ( D) =         3,000
103                    setup cost in dollars (Co) =    $2,500.00
104  carrying cost in dollars per year per unit (Ch) =      $7.00
105                   annual poduction capacity ( P) =      10000
106           number of operating days per year ( T) =        365
107                                 Lead time ( L) =         21
108
109                     economic lot size (ELS) =       1749.64
110           length of a production run in days =         63.86
111                           minimum total cost =        $8,573
112                               reorder point =        172.60
113                     production runs per year =          1.71
114                           cycle time in days =        212.37
115                           maximum inventory =       1224.74
116
117
118
119
10-Feb-90   10:36 AM                      CMD
```

Additional Options

1. From the main menu, you may choose the EDIT option which allows you to change any of the input data and recompute the ELS and cost.

2. You may also select GRAPH, which displays a graph of the relevant costs similar to that in the EOQ template.

TEXT EXERCISES

1. All-Star Bat Manufacturing, Inc., supplies baseball bats to major and minor league baseball teams.   After an initial order in January, demand over the 6-month baseball season is approximately constant at 1000 bats per month. Assuming that the bat production process can handle up to 4000 bats per month, the bat production setup costs are $150 per setup, the production cost is $10 per bat, and assuming that All-Star uses a 2 percent monthly inventory holding cost, what production lot size would you recommend to meet the demand during the baseball season? If All-Star operates 20 days per month, how often will the production process operate, and what is the length of a production run? (Chapter 3, page 569, problem 12).

2. Suppose that D = 6400 units per year, Co = $100, and Ch = $2 per unit per year.   Compute the minimum-cost production lot size for each of the following production rates:

    a.   8000 units per year

    b.   10,000 units per year

    c.   32,000 units per year

    d.   100,000 units per year

    Also, compute the economic order quantity.   What two observations can you make about the relationship between the EOQ model and the production lot size model? (Chapter 13, problem 13, page 569).

3. Wilson Publishing Company produces books for the retail market. Demand for a current book is expected to occur at a constant annual rate of 7200 copies. The cost of one copy of the book is $14.50. Inventory holding costs are based on an 18 percent annual rate, and production setup costs are $150 per setup. The equipment the book is produced on has an annual production volume of 25,000 copies. There are 250 working days per year and the lead time for a production run is 15 days. Use the production lot-size model to compute the following values:

    a. minimum-cost production lot size

    b. number of production runs per year

    c. cycle time

    d. length of a production run

    e. maximum inventory level

    f. total annual cost

    g. reorder point

    (Chapter 13, Problem 14, Page 569)

4. A well-known manufacturer of several brands of toothpaste uses the production lot-size model to determine production quantities for its various products. The product known as Extra White is currently being produced in production lot sizes of 5000 units. The length of the production run for this quantity is 10 days. Because of a recent shortage of

a particular raw material, the supplier of the material has announced a cost increase that will be passed along to the manufacturer of Extra White. Current estimates are that the new raw material cost will increase the manu-facturing cost of the toothpaste products by 23 percent per unit. What will be the effect of this price increase on the production lot sizes for Extra White?

(Chapter 13, Problem 15, Page 569)

SUPPLEMENTARY EXERCISES

1. One of the product lines MARKAL produces is brass greeting cards. The company expects next year's demand for greeting cards to be 20,000 at a uniform rate. It costs $100 to set up the equipment to produce the brass greeting cards and the production rate is 4000 per month. It costs $0.50 per year to hold a greeting card in inventory. What is the Economic Lot Size for production? What is the maximum inventory carried during the year?

2. Pittsburgh Textile Mills produces a variety of special ties for men, which is demanded at the annual rate of 180,000 ties (250 days). The manufacturing process set up cost is $150 and at a daily rate of production of 3000 ties per day. The carryig cost for a tie is $0.50 per year.

    a. Calculate the economic lot size.

b.   What is the length of the production run for this lot size?

c.   Assuming initial inventory of zero, what is the maximum inventory?

3.   Kane's Furniture has an annual demand rate of 1,000 units and an annual production capacity of 2000 units. The set-up and holding costs are $10 and $1.00 respectively. What is the economic lot size for units to be produced each time?

4.   Midori's Bicycle Shop has an annual demand of 5000 units. The average price of a bicycle is $60. Set-up costs total $40 and the carrying costs are 25% of the price per unit per year. The company produces these bicycles in a shop behind its display, customer, and sales offices. There is a six-day lead time between the order receipt and final assembly. The rate of production is 60 bicycles/day, and the shop operates 250 days per year. What is the economic lot-size for produciton? What is the total inventory cost and the reorder point?

Chapter 9
AGGREGATE PLANNING

Introduction

Aggregate production planning is the development of monthly or quarterly production requirements for product groups or families that will meet the estimates of demand. Strategies for dealing with fluctuating demand include production rate changes, work force changes, inventory smoothing, and demand shifting. The choice of strategy depends on corporate policies, practical limitations, and cost factors. Aggregate planning is discussed in Section 14.2 of the text.

Using the Aggregate Planning Template

To illustrate the use fo the template, we will use the Golden Breweries example discussed in Chapter 14. The table below gives a monthly aggregate demand forecast over the next year.

Month	Demand (Barrels)	Cumulative Demand
January	1,500	1,500
February	1,000	2,500
March	1,900	4,400
April	2,600	7,000
May	2,800	9,800
June	3,100	12,900
July	3,200	16,100
August	3,000	19,100
September	2,000	21,100
October	1,000	22,100
November	1,800	23,900
December	2,200	26,100

Let us suppose that Golden Breweries has a normal production capacity of 2200 barrels per month and a current inventory of 1000 barrels. Assume that the production cost is $70 per barrel, inventory-holding costs amount to $1.40 per barrel per month of ending inventory, lost sales have an opportunity cost of $90 per barrel, overtime costs $6.50 additional per barrel, and there is a $5 per barrel charge to change the production rate. Cost of undertime (production below full capacity) is $3.00 per barrel. For a production at normal capacity, we seek to develop a production/inventory plan at full capacity.

After you have invoked the aggregate planning template from the main menu, the following screen will appear:

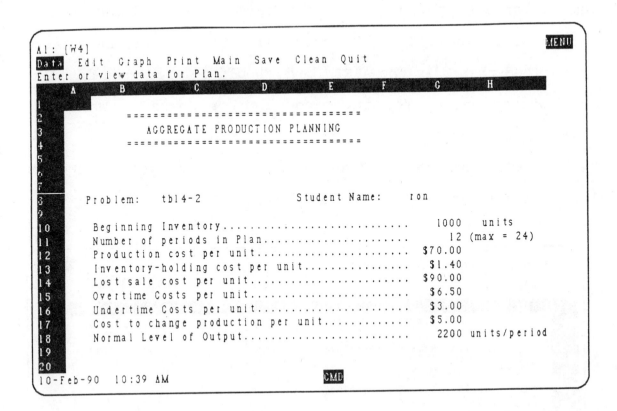

```
A1: [W4]                                                        MENU
Data  Edit  Graph  Print  Main  Save  Clean  Quit
Enter or view data for Plan.
      A       B       C       D       E       F       G       H
1
2
3              ===================================
4                  AGGREGATE PRODUCTION PLANNING
5              ===================================
6
7
8       Problem:   tbl4-2              Student Name:    ron
9
10        Beginning Inventory.........................    1000    units
11        Number of periods in Plan...................      12  (max = 24)
12        Production cost per unit....................  $70.00
13        Inventory-holding cost per unit.............   $1.40
14        Lost sale cost per unit.....................  $90.00
15        Overtime Costs per unit.....................   $6.50
16        Undertime Costs per unit....................   $3.00
17        Cost to change production per unit..........   $5.00
18        Normal Level of Output......................    2200  units/period
19
20
10-Feb-90  10:39 AM                     CMD
```

To begin, select DATA from the main menu. You will be
prompted first for the problem name and your name. Next, enter
the parameters of the problem. Use the ENTER key after each
response.

Beginning inventory .... 1000 units
Number of periods in plan 12
Production cost per unit $70.00
Inventory-holding cost per unit $1.40
Lost sale cost per unit $90.00
Overtime cost per unit $6.50
Undertime cost per unit $3.00
Cost to change production/unit $5.00
Normal Level of Output .... 2200 units/period

After inputting the normal level of output, press the ENTER

key and a screen will be displayed in which you will enter the demand for each period. Move the cursor to the demand column and enter the demand for each period. Once again, it must be emphasized that only the ARROW keys should be used when entering or changing values for the production or demand. When completed, this screen will look like Table 14.3 and is shown below. Note that the cumulative production is not adjusted for lost sales as it is in Table 14.3.

```
AB105:  U [W10]  +$NORM PROD                                              READY

            AA        AB        AC        AD        AE        AF        AG        AH
101                        Inventory Plan
102                                                                  -Cumulative-
103             Production  Demand   Inventory            Lost      Prod.    Demand
104    Prd.                                              Sales
105       1        2200      1500      1700               0          3200     1500
106       2        2200      1000      2900               0          5400     2500
107       3        2200      1900      3200               0          7600     4400
108       4        2200      2600      2800               0          9800     7000
109       5        2200      2800      2200               0         12000     9800
110       6        2200      3100      1300               0         14200    12900
111       7        2200      3200       300               0         16400    16100
112       8        2200      3000         0             500         18600    19100
113       9        2200      2000       200               0         20800    21100
114      10        2200      1000      1400               0         23000    22100
115      11        2200      1800      1800               0         25200    23900
116      12        2200      2200      1800               0         27400    26100
117             --------  --------  --------        --------
118               26400     26100                       500
119
120                    Total Plan Cost . . $1,920,440
10-Feb-90   10:40 AM                         CMD
```

When you press ENTER next, the screen will display the cost calculations similar to Table 14.1 on page 584. This is shown below.

```
A101: U [W4]                                                          READY

        A      B         C          D         E       F      G         H
100        Problem: tbl4-2                Student Name:     ron
101                   Cost Calculation for Production Plan
102                                                                 Rate
103       Production Production   Ending         Inv.  --Lost Sales- Change
104    Prd.             Cost   Inventor      Cost Number    Cost    Cost
105     1      2200    $154,000    1700    $2,380     0      $0       -
106     2      2200    $154,000    2900    $4,060     0      $0       -
107     3      2200    $154,000    3200    $4,480     0      $0       -
108     4      2200    $154,000    2800    $3,920     0      $0       -
109     5      2200    $154,000    2200    $3,080     0      $0       -
110     6      2200    $154,000    1300    $1,820     0      $0       -
111     7      2200    $154,000     300      $420     0      $0       -
112     8      2200    $154,000       0       $0    500   $45,000     -
113     9      2200    $154,000     200      $280     0      $0       -
114    10      2200    $154,000    1400    $1,960     0      $0       -
115    11      2200    $154,000    1800    $2,520     0      $0       -
116    12      2200    $154,000    1800    $2,520     0      $0       -
117           --------  --------- --------  -------- ------ -------- -------
118          26400   $1,848,000          $27,440   500   $45,000      $0
119
10-Feb-90   10:41 AM                      CMD
```

PLEASE NOTE THAT OVERTIME AND UNDERTIME COST COLUMNS ARE
"HIDDEN" FROM THE SCREEN.   TO VIEW THESE COLUMNS, USE THE RIGHT
AND LEFT ARROW KEYS TO MOVE FROM THE CURRENT SCREEN.   You will
see the screen as shown below.

```
J101: U                                                                    READY

           C         D           E        F        G       H        I        J
100  tbl4-2                 Student Name:      ron
101   Cost Calculation for Production Plan
102                                                      Rate     Over-    Under-
103  Production  Ending          Inv.    --Lost Sales- Change    Time      Time
104       Cost Inventor        Cost Number     Cost    Cost     Cost     Cost
105    $154,000   1700       $2,380      0       $0      -        -        -
106    $154,000   2900       $4,060      0       $0      -        -        -
107    $154,000   3200       $4,480      0       $0      -        -        -
108    $154,000   2800       $3,920      0       $0      -        -        -
109    $154,000   2200       $3,080      0       $0      -        -        -
110    $154,000   1300       $1,820      0       $0      -        -        -
111    $154,000    300        $420       0       $0      -        -        -
112    $154,000      0         $0      500    $45,000    -        -        -
113    $154,000    200        $280       0       $0      -        -        -
114    $154,000   1400       $1,960      0       $0      -        -        -
115    $154,000   1800       $2,520      0       $0      -        -        -
116    $154,000   1800       $2,520      0       $0      -        -        -
117    --------  --------    --------  ------  -------  -------  -------  -------
118  $1,848,000             $27,440    500    $45,000    $0       $0       $0
119
10-Feb-90   10:41 AM                           CMD
```

Additional Options

1. From the DATA submenu, you may select COST-VIEW or PLAN-VIEW. These selections will display the cost calculations or the inventory plan, respectively.

2. Selecting the GRAPH option from the menu will display a graph of the cumulative production and cumulative demand curves, similar to that in Figure 14.3 on page 585.

3. From the EDIT option, you may choose to edit PARAMETERS or PRODUCTION data.   The PARAMETERS option allows you to change any of the data entered in the opening screen.   The PRODUCTION option allows you to change individual values of production or demand in the Inventory Plan screen.   In this way, you can

perform scenario analyses such as the one illustrated in Table 14.6 on page 586.

TEXT EXERCISES

1. Consider the following six-month demand forecast:

Month	Jul	Aug	Sep	Oct	Nov	Dec
Forecast	850	900	1000	850	600	450

a. Compute the cumulative demand for each month and the average demand per month.

b. If the production for each month is set equal to the average demand, compute the net ending inventory for each month, assuming that the ending inventory for June is 150 units, and that all shortages are backordered.

c. Draw a graph of cumulative production and cumulative demand.

(Chapter 14, problem 1, page 600)

2. A manufacturer of stamped metal parts has a sales forecast for the next 5 weeks of a particular part.

Week	1	2	3	4	5
Forecast	2000	2500	3000	3000	3500

Beginning inventory equals 13,000 units and the firm wishes to maintain this level at the end of the planning period.

a. What weekly production rate is necessary?

b. Suppose the company wishes to reduce its inventory level

to 10,000 units, how would the production plan change?
(Chapter 14, problem 2, page 601)

3. The projected aggregate demand of a certain product is given
    for the next 12 months.   What is the minimum level of
    constant production necessary to meet demand and incur no
    stockouts?   Assume an initial inventory of 150.   Show your
    results on a graph.

Month	1	2	3	4	5	6
Demand	480	530	500	480	470	520

Month	7	8	9	10	11	12
Demand	450	480	500	530	570	600

(Chapter 14, problem 3, page 601)

4. Chapman Pharmaceuticals, a large manufacturer of drugs, has
    an aggregate demand forecast for a liquid cold medicine.

Month	J	F	M	A	M	J
Liters (1000s)	180	120	75	60	20	15

Month	J	A	S	O	N	D
Liters (1000s)	15	15	30	70	90	150

a.   If the firm has a capacity of 80 thousand liters per
month, show by means of a graph the sales level, production
level, and inventory level over the next 12 months if the

initial inventory is 190,000 liters.

b.   What is the minimum level of production necessary to maintain a nonnegative inventory?

c.   Develop a plan that includes overtime for which inventory levels are held to at least a 100,000 liter level each month.

(Chapter 14, problem 4, page 601)

5.   For Chapman Pharmaceuticals in Problem 4, suppose that inventory holding costs are $25 per 1000 liters per month, regular time production costs are $350 per 1000 liters, and overtime premiums add an additional 20 percent. Compute the cost of the production plans developed in parts (a) and (c) in Problem 4. (Chapter 14, problem 5, page 601).

6.   Refer to Chapman Pharmaceuticals in Problems 4 and 5. Suppose that normal capacity is 80,000 liters per month and a maximum of 20,000 liters can be produced in overtime. If the initial inventory in January is 150,000 liters and there are no other inventory restrictions, provide an optimum production/inventory plan.   (Chapter 14, problem 6, page 601).

7.   Determine a more cost-effective production plan than the one indicated above for Golden Breweries that incurs no shortages.   (Chapter 14, problem 7, page 602).

8. Given the following monthly demand pattern and unit produc-
    tion cost of $1.20, overtime costs of $1.30 per unit, and
    subcontracting costs of $1.40 per unit compute the cost of
    a level production strategy and also a strategy of setting
    production levels equal to the monthly demand.   The
    inventory holding cost is $0.20 per unit per month.   In the
    case of level production strategy, assume a desired ending
    inventory of 24,000. The beginning inventory for both cases
    is 20,000 units.   The capacity for regular production is
    24,000 units and there is an
    overtime capacity of 2000 units and a subcontracting
    option up to 2000 units.

Month	1	2	3	4	5	6
Demand (1000s)	24	22	26	20	20	20

Month	7	8	9	10	11	12
Demand (1000s)	22	23	24	26	28	28

(Chapter 14, problem 8, page 602)

9. The Westerbeck Co. manufactures several models of washers
    and dryers. The projected requirements over the next year
    for their automatic washers are

Month	Jan	Feb	Mar	Apr	May	June
Requirement	800	1030	810	900	950	1340

Month	Jul	Aug	Sep	Oct	Nov	Dec
Requirement	1100	1210	600	580	890	1000

Current inventory is 100 units. The firm's current capacity is 960 units per month. The average salary of production workers is $1300 per month. Overtime is paid at time and one-half up to 20 percent additional time. Each production worker accounts for 30 units per month. Additional labor can be hired for a training cost of $250. and existing workers can be laid off at a cost of $500. Any increase or decrease in the production rate costs
$5000 for tooling, setup, and line charges. This does not apply, however, to overtime. Inventory holding costs are $25 per unit per month. Backorders cost $75 per unit short. Determine at least two different production plans, trying to minimize the cost of meeting the next year's requirements. (Chapter 14, problem 9, page 602).

CASE PROBLEM

A small manufacturer of marine radios has the following quarterly sales data for the past 7 years:

Year	Quarter				Total Sales
	1	2	3	4	
1	60	150	100	40	350
2	100	180	150	70	500
3	140	260	230	120	750
4	190	280	250	180	900
5	220	340	280	210	1050
6	240	360	300	200	1100
7	280	400	350	270	1300

a. Show the four-quarter, moving-average values for this time series. Plot this along with the original time series.

b. Develop a quarterly forecast for next year using either a moving-average or an exponential forecasting technique.

c. The plant has a capacity to manufacture 130 radios per month. Develop three alternate monthly production plans for the next year, assuming there are 80 radios currently in inventory. Show your results graphically and in tabular form. Include a discussion of safety stock, overtime, rate changes, and so on. What if forecasts are off by 10 percent on the low side? Which of your plans would appear to be best? (Chapter 14, case problem, page 605).

SUPPLEMENTARY EXERCISES

1. The Shamking Company manufactures various types of electr-
    onic calculators. The projected requirements over the next
    year for their solar-powered calculators are:

Month	Requiremements
Jan	750
Feb	970
Mar	810
Apr	900
May	960
June	1010
July	1200
Aug	1300
Sep	1500
Oct	1200
Nov	990
Dec	900

Current inventory is 200 units. The firm's current capacity
is 1000 units per month. The average salary of production
workers is $1500 per month. Overtime is paid at time and
one-half. Each employee currently has a normal productivity
of 40 units per month. Storage costs per unit are $1.50 per
month. Shortages are $10.00 per unit short on inventory.
The cost of hiring and training a new employee are $300.
Layoff costs are $400 per employee. Subcontractors can be
hired to raise capacity at a cost of $15.00 per unit. Using
this data, establish an aggregate output plan for next year.
Use a constant production strategy.

2. The Jayrad Company manufactures various types of portable
    radios. The projected demand for the coming year is as

follows:

Month	Demand
Jan	700
Feb	900
Mar	800
Apr	1000
May	960
June	1200
July	1250
Aug	1300
Sep	1400
Oct	1250
Nov	950
Dec	890

Current inventory is 150 units. The firm's current capacity is 1050 units per month. The average salary of production workers is $1300 per month. Overtime is paid at time and onehalf. Each employee currently has a normal productivity of 30 units per month. Storage costs per unit are $1.00 per month. Shortages are $9.00 per unit short on inventory. The cost of hiring and training a new employee are $250. Layoff costs are $300 per employee. Subcontractors can be hired to raise capacity at a cost of $20.00 per unit. Using this data, establish a production plan for next year, setting production rate equal to demand rate.

3. The MARKAL Corporation has established its aggregate demand for the coming year as follows:

Month	Productive Days	Demand (units)
Jan	21	8,000
Feb	20	10,000
Mar	22	19,000
Apr	21	20,000
May	20	29,000
Jun	19	24,000
Jul	20	27,000
Aug	11	15,000
Sep	20	19,000
Oct	22	13,000
Nov	18	8,000
Dec	21	9,000

Each employee has a normal productivity of 11 units per day. By working overtime, daily capacity can be increased by up to 25 percent at an additional cost of $3.00 per unit. The employees' daily average salaries are $35.00.

Storage costs are per unit are $1.00 per month. Shortages are valued at $9.00 per unit short on inventory. The costs of hiring and training a new employee are $250.00. Layoff costs are $225 per employee. Subcontractors can be hired to raise capacity at a cost of $10.00 per unit. Starting inventory for MARKAL is 5,000 units. Using this data, establish an aggregate production plan for next year.

Chapter 10
MATERIAL REQUIREMENTS
PLANNING (MRP)

<u>Introduction</u>

Material Requirements Planning (MRP) is a technique used to plan for and control manufacturing inventories. MRP uses information contained in a bill of materials, the master production schedule, and current inventory records to perform time-phasing calculations for components and subassemblies. MRP calculations determines the net requirements and planned order releases for all components and subassemblies over some time horizon. Further discussions of MRP are contained in Chapter 15 of the text.

<u>Using the Material Requirements Planning Template</u>

We shall illustrate the MRP template with the Spiecker manufacturing example found in chapter 14, page 466 of the text. The following figure shows the Bill of Material (BOM) for the 14 inch snowblower.

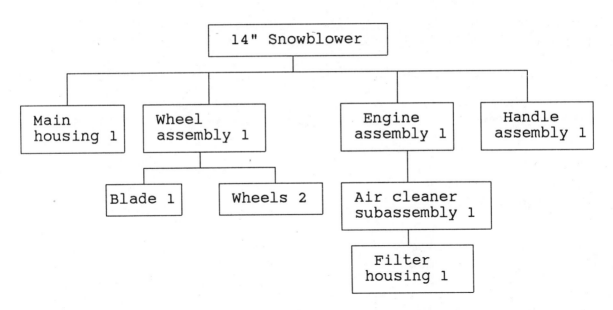

Suppose that the Master Production Schedule (MPS) calls for the final asssembly of 1250 units of the 14 inch snowblower during week 12 of the current planning period. (The template can handle up to 12 buckets; thus we have changed the text example slightly to account for this). The time required to assemble the four main assemblies of the snowblower is 1 week. The accompanying table gives the production lead times for the remaining components and assemblies.

COMPONENT OR ASSEMBLY	LEAD TIME (WEEKS)
Main housing assembly	3
Wheel assembly	1
Blade assembly	2
Wheels	1
Engine assembly	4
Air cleaner subassembly	1
Filter housing	2
Handle assembly	1

The following table gives the current inventory levels

for each component or assembly.

```
--------------------------------------------------------
  COMPONENT OR ASSEMBLY          INVENTORY
--------------------------------------------------------
  Main housing assembly             400

  Wheel assembly                    200
    Blade assembly                  800
    Wheels                         2300

  Engine assembly                   450
    Air cleaner assembly            250
    Filter housing                  500

  Handle assembly                   400

--------------------------------------------------------
```

After you have invoked the MRP template from the main menu,

the following screen will appear:

```
 A1: [W7]                                                        MENU
Data  Edit/view  Print  Main  Save  Quit
Enter data for Plan.
       A    B   C   D E F  G     H     I     J     K     L    M     N
 1
 2           ----------------------------------------
 3           MRP (Materials Requirements Planning)
 4           ----------------------------------------
 5
 6
 7
 8     Problem:   ------------Student Name:         --------------
 9
10        Contents:   Sample format.
11       *******************************************************
12       *                End Item                             *
13       *  Assembly-A  Assembly-B  Assembly-C  Assembly-D     *
14       *  Sub-A1      Sub-B1      Sub-C1      Sub-D1         *
15       *  Sub-A2      Sub-B2      Sub-C2      Sub-D2         *
16       *  Cmp1-Sub-A1 Cmp1-Sub-B1 Cmp1-Sub-C2 Cmp1-Sub-D2   *
17       *  Cmp2-Sub-A1 Cmp2-Sub-B1 Cmp2-Sub-C2 Cmp2-Sub-D2   *
18       *                                                     *
19       *******************************************************
20
 23-Feb-90   10:16 AM                      CMD         CALC
```

The input of the data in this template is quite different from other templates due to the nature of MRP. The basic flow of information comes from the bill of material structure. This is illustrated by the following diagram.

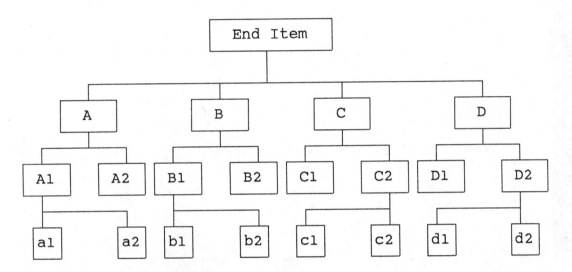

This figure shows the maximum size of a bill of material structure that can be accommodated with the template. That is, you may have at most four assemblies (A, B, C, and D); each assembly may have at most two sub-assemblies (A1 and A2, B1 and B2, and so on); and each sub-assembly may have at most one component (a1, a2, and so on). The Spieker snowblower example falls within these restrictions.

Select DATA from the menu, type in the problem name and your name, using the ENTER key after each response. After entering your name, you will see a new menu at the top of the screen:

END-ITEM ASSEMBLY-A ASSEMBLY-B ASSEMBLY-C ASSEMBLY-D MAIN

(see the figure below)

```
K8: U 'Student                                                    MENU
End-Item  Assembly-A  Assembly-B  Assembly-C  Assembly-D  Main
Input or Edit data for End Item.
       A    B    C    D E F G    H    I    J    K    L    M    N

              ============================================
              MRP (Materials Requirements Planning)
              ============================================


     Problem:    Sample       Student Name:      Student

        Contents:   Sample format.
      ***************************************************
      *                      End Item                    *
      *  Assembly-A   Assembly-B   Assembly-C   Assembly-D  *
      *  Sub-A1       Sub-B1       Sub-C1       Sub-D1      *
      *  Sub-A2       Sub-B2       Sub-C2       Sub-D2      *
      *  Comp-Sub-A1  Comp-Sub-B1  Comp-Sub-C2  Comp-Sub-D2 *
      *  Comp-Sub-A1  Comp-Sub-B1  Comp-Sub-C2  Comp-Sub-D2 *
      *                                                     *
      ***************************************************

10-Feb-90   10:42 AM                      NUM        CALC
```

This menu allows you to select the end item or one of the four assemblies for which to enter the data. The input data needed for MRP reports are: Gross Requirements (GR), Scheduled Receipts (SR), On Hand Inventory (OH), Number of assemblies, sub-assemblies or components required for each parent item, and Lead Time (LT). The template will calculate the Net Requirements (NR) and Planned Order Releases (POR) for each item.

First select END-ITEM from the menu. The following screen will appear:

	End Item	xxxxxxxxxxxxxxxxxx						
	Prd	0	1	2	3	4	5	6	7
	Qty								
End	GR		0	0	0	0	0	0	0
Item	SR		0	0	0	0	0	0	0
	OH	0	0	0	0	0	0	0	0
LT=	NR		0	0	0	0	0	0	0
0	POR		NA	NA	NA	NA	NA	NA	NA

The cursor will be positioned initially at "xxxxxxxxxxxx". At this point, type in the name of the end-item. Use the right ARROW key to move the cursor to the "Prd. Qty." line. For each period, type in the number of end items required in each period (this is the Master Production Schedule data). The screen has room for only seven time periods to be displayed. However, if you continue to move the right ARROW key you will see the remaining periods (up to 12). The number of end items required will automatically be entered in the GR (gross requirements) row. Moving the right ARROW will position the cursor next to the SR (scheduled receipts) row. Enter any scheduled receipts for the item in the appropriate cells. Move all the way through the row even if there are no scheduled receipts. Finally, enter the initial inventory (OH row for period 0) and the lead time in the appropriate cells. Press the ENTER key and the previous menu will return.

You may now select ASSEMBLY-A, ASSEMBLY-B, and so on to enter the appropriate data in a similar manner. The only difference in the assembly screens is the inclusion of the data element "0 times" in the initial MRP matrix. In this cell, enter the number of that assembly or component required for each parent item.

Continue this data input process for each sub-assembly or component. When you have finished inputting the data for a particular assembly, press ENTER and the menu will return, allowing you to select another assembly. When all the data have been entered, you may select any of the menu items to view the final MRP calculations or MAIN to return to main menu. This will allow you to print or save the results.

Additional Options

1. From the main menu, you may select EDIT/VIEW to either change any data or view the calculations.

TEXT EXERCISES

1. For the Spiecker Manufacturing example, determine the net requirements for the engine assembly, the air cleaner subassembly, and the filter housing if the number of units in inventory are 500, 375, and 250, respectively. Assume that 1250 units of the 14-inch snowblower are still required in week 9. (Chapter 15, problem 1, page 654).

2. For the Spiecker example, determine the effect on time phasing if lead times are 5 for the engine assembly, 2 for the air cleaner subassembly, and 3 for the filter housing.

(Chapter 15, problem 2, page 654)

3. An electrical appliance A consists of three major subas-
    semblies: B, C, and D.   One unit of A is comprised of 2
    units of B, 1 unit of C, and 3 units of D.   The subassembly
    B consists of 2 units of D, 1 unit of E, and 1 unit of F.
    The subassembly C consists of 2 units of E.   The subassembly
    D, consists of 1 unit of E and 1 unit of F.   A second major
    appliance G consists of 3 units of D and 4 units of F.
    a.   Draw the bill of materials for products A and G.
    b.   If 50 units of A and 25 units of G are required for the
    month of May, compute the requirements of all components and
    subassemblies.

    (Chapter 15, problem 3, page 655)

4. In problem 3, suppose that 100 units of A and 50 units of
    G are required for the month of June.   At the end of May,
    we have the following stock on hand:

Item	A	G	B	C	D	E	F
Stock on hand	50	25	50	20	350	0	175

    Calculate the requirements for all components and subas-
    semblies. (Chapter 15, problem 4, page 655).

5. C&D Lawn Products manufactures a rotary spreader for
    applying fertilizer.   A portion of the BOM is shown

in the figure below.

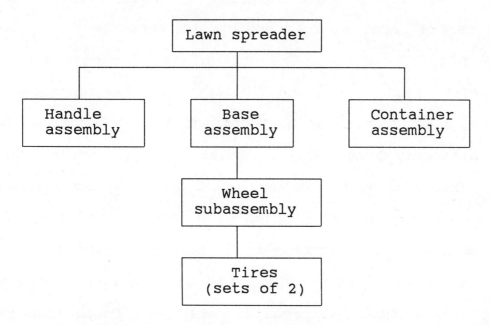

If 3000 lawn spreaders are needed to satisfy a customer's order, determine the net requirements for the base assembly, and tires. Assume that 1000, 1500, and 800 of each component are currently in inventory. (Chapter 15, problem 5, page 655).

6. In problem 5, assume that the lead time for the base assembly, wheel subassembly, and tires are 2, 4, and 5 weeks, respectively. If all components must be completed no later than week 10 of the current production period, determine when orders must be placed to meet the production schedule. (Chapter 15, problem 6, page 655)

SUPPLEMENTARY EXERCISES

1. For the following bill of materials and data, construct an
    MRP schedule.

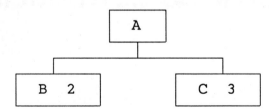

The master production schedule calls for 40 units of A each
week for 8 weeks. The lead time for assembling the end item
A is negligible; the lead times for components B and C are
1 and 3 weeks respectively.   On hand inventories for
components B and C are 240 and 600.

2. For the same bill of materials structure in supplementary
    problem 1, suppose that the master production schedule calls
    for 600 units of A in week 5 and 600 units in week 10. Lead
    times and on-hand inventories are the same. However, 200
    units of component B are scheduled to be received in weeks
    3, 6, and 9. What is the material requirements plan for
    this situation?

Chapter 11
OPERATIONS SCHEDULING

Introduction

In a job shop, several jobs must be processed, each of which may have a different routing among departments or machines in the shop. An important decision involves scheduling and sequencing the jobs. Scheduling is the process of assigning starting and completion times to jobs; sequencing involves the determination of the order in which jobs are processed. Performance measures include average completion time, average job lateness, and average number of jobs in the system.

The simplest scheduling problem is that of processing n jobs on a single processor. Jobs can be sequenced in any order. Scheduling rules which seek to optimize some measure of performance are often employed. Two common scheduling rules are shortest processing time (SPT) and earliest due date (EDD).

Using the Job Shop Scheduling Template

To illustrate the use of the template, we will use the Sequencing by Shortest Processing Time and Sequencing by Earliest Due Date examples discussed in Chapter 16 on pages 667-669. The shortest processing rule does not consider due dates; hence it may be applied to problems which do not involve due dates.

Let us assume that six machines are scheduled to be repaired, with estimated repair times given below. No new jobs are scheduled to arrive.

Job	Processing Time (Hr)
1	8
2	4
3	7
4	3
5	6
6	5

In what order would the jobs be processed using the SPT rule?

After you have invoked the operations scheduling template from the main menu, the following screen will appear:

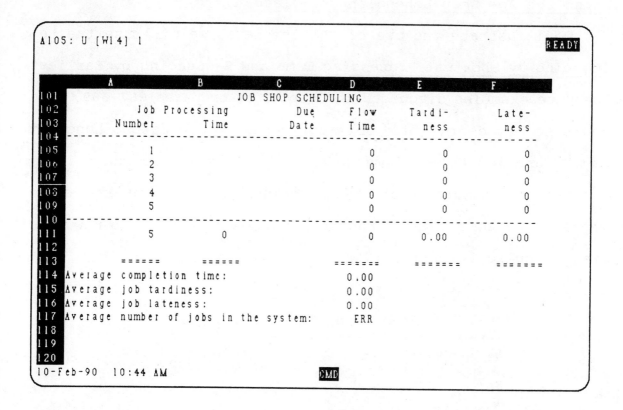

To begin, select DATA followed by NEW DATA. The template will prompt you for the problem title, your name, and number of jobs to be scheduled. Press ENTER after typing each response. The second screen will then appear in which you will enter the processing time and, if applicable, due dates.

Using the ARROW keys, input the processing time for each job. You will have the following results:

```
+------------------------------------------------------------+
|          JOB SHOP SCHEDULING                               |
|                                                            |
|    Job  Processing      Due     Flow  Tardi- Late-         |
| Number       Time      Date     Time   ness  ness          |
|                                                            |
|      1          8                  8      8     8          |
|      2          4                 12     12    12          |
|      3          7                 19     19    19          |
|      4          3                 22     22    22          |
|      5          6                 28     28    28          |
|      6          5                 33     33    33          |
|  ------------------------------------------------------     |
|      6         33                122    122   122          |
|                                                            |
| Average completion time:            20.33                  |
| Average job tardiness:              20.33                  |
| Average job lateness:               20.33                  |
| Average number of jobs in the system:  3.70                |
+------------------------------------------------------------+
```

Since there are no due dates, ignore the information contained in the Tardiness and Lateness columns are not relevant to this example. Just ignore them. The flow times and statistics are computed for the sequence as shown, namely 1 - 2 - 3 - 4 - 5 - 6. You may change the sequence of job numbers and processing times to any order that you desire. To obtain the SPT sequence, press ENTER to return to the opening screen and select ANALYZE. From this submenu, select PROCESSING TIME. The following screen will be shown.

```
                    JOB SHOP SCHEDULING

    Job   Processing      Due      Flow   Tardi- Late-
  Number       Time       Date     Time    ness   ness

      4           3                   3       3      3
      2           4                   7       7      7
      6           5                  12      12     12
      5           6                  18      18     18
      3           7                  25      25     25
      1           8                  33      33     33
  -----------------------------------------------------
      6          33                  98      98     98

  Average completion time:          16.33
  Average job tardiness:            16.33
  Average job lateness:             16.33
  Average number of jobs in the system:  2.97
```

To illustrate an example with due dates, consider the example on page 668. Suppose that five jobs have processing times and due dates as given below:

```
  -------------------------------------
  Job  Processing Time    Due Date
  -------------------------------------
   1           4               15
   2           7               16
   3           2                8
   4           6               21
   5           3                9
  -------------------------------------
```

Schedule the jobs using the earliest due date rule. After inputting the data, select the DUE DATE option from the ANALYZE submenu. The following results will be shown.

```
              JOB SHOP SCHEDULING

   Job   Processing      Due     Flow   Tardi- Late-
 Number        Time      Date    Time    ness   ness

    3           2          8       2       0    - 6
    5           3          9       5       0    - 4
    1           4         15       9       0    - 6
    2           7         16      16       0      0
    4           6         21      22       1      1
 ------------------------------------------------------
    5          22                 54       1    -15

 Average completion time:              10.80
 Average job tardiness:                 0.20
 Average job lateness:                 -3.00
 Average number of jobs in the system:  2.45
```

Additional Options

1. From the DATA menu option, you may select EXTEND DATA, which allows you to enter additional jobs to a problem, or EDIT, which allows you to change the data.

2. From the ANALYZE menu option, you may choose to sequence the jobs by either first-in, first served; shortest processing time; or earliest due date. The SUMMARY option displays a summary of the average completion time, average lateness, and average number of jobs in the system for each of the three sequencing rules.

TEXT EXERCISES

1. The following 6 jobs are to be scheduled on a single machine.

Job	1	2	3	4	5	6
Processing Time (min)	240	120	210	90	180	150

a.   Suppose the jobs are processed in numerical order. Compute the average flowtime after each job is completed.

b.   In what order would the jobs be processed using the SPT rule?   Compute the average flowtime after each job is completed.   Compare this answer with your answer to part (a).

c.   In what sense does SPT minimize the average flow time? Why would this rule be preferred?   (Chapter 16, page 697, problem 4).

2.   Five jobs are waiting to be processed on a single machine. Use the shortest processing time rule to sequence the jobs. Compute the flowtime and lateness for each job.   Also, compute the average flowtime and average lateness for all jobs.

Job	Processing time	Due date
1	7	20
2	3	8
3	5	7
4	2	4
5	6	17

(Chapter 16, page 698, problem 5)

3. Schedule the jobs in Problem 5 using the earliest due date rule. How do the performance measure compare with the SPT rule? (Chapter 16, page 698, problem 6).

4. Tony's Income Tax Service personnel can estimate the time required to complete tax forms using standards for each particular form which must be filed. These are as follows.

Form	Standard Time (min)
1040 short	10
1040 long	15
Schedule A	15
Schedule B	5
Schedule G	10
Schedule C	15
Schedule SE	5
Form 2106	10

One morning, five customers are waiting:

Customer	Forms
A	1040 long, schedules A,B
B	1040 long, schedules A,B,SE, 2106
C	1040 short
D	1040 long, schedules A,B, G
E	1040 long, schedules A,B,C, 2106

a. If these customers are processed on a first-come first-served basis, what is the flowtime of each and the average flowtime?

b. If SPT is used, how will the flowtimes change? (Chapter 16, page 698, problem 7).

SUPPLEMENTARY EXERCISES

1. SHILA industries has a job shop manufacturing facility which processes jobs to customer orders. Currently six open orders are awaiting processing.

Orders to be processed (in order of arrival)	A	B	C	D	E	F
Processing time (days)	19	15	23	20	11	9
Due date (days from now)		30	19	33	28	19	12

a. Apply the first-come first-served (FCFS) priority sequencing rule to the SHILA facility. Calculate the total completion time, average completion time, average number of jobs per day in the system, and average job lateness.

b. Apply the shortest processing time (SPT) rule and perform the same calculations as in part a.

2. For problem 1, use the earliest due date rule and calculate the total completion time, average completion time, average number of jobs per day in the system, and average job lateness.

3. L&R Industries has a job shop service facility which provides interior decorations for a variety of commercial and family units. Currently six open orders are awaiting processing.

Orders to be processed (in order of arrival)	G	H	I	J	K	L
Processing time (days)	20	18	25	22	15	17
Due date (days from now)	25	20	30	27	29	19

a. Apply the shortest processing (SPT) priority sequencing rule to the L&R industries. Provide the following statistics: average completion time and average job lateness.

b. Apply the first-come first-served (FCFS) priority sequencing rule and perform the same calculations as in part a.

4. In exercise 3, due to changes in the specifications, order K will require 19 days to process and the due date remains the same. Provide your revised schedules for parts a and b.

Chapter 12
CONTROL CHART FOR VARIABLES

Introduction

Variables refer to those characteristics that can be measured on a continuous scale; for instance, length or weight. With variable measurement, we are concerned with the degree of conformance to specifications. The charts that are most commonly used for variable data are the X-bar chart and R-chart (or range chart). The X-bar chart is used to depict the variation in the centering of the process, and the R-chart is used to depict the variation in the ranges of the samples. Control charts for variables is discussed in Section 19.6 of the text.

Using the Control Chart for Variables Template

To illustrate the use of the template, we will use the Goodman Tire and Rubber Company example discussed in page 809 of the text. The company periodically tests its tires for tread

wear under simulated road conditions. To study and control its
manufacturing processes, the company uses X-bar and R-charts.
Twenty samples, each containing three radial tires, were chosen
from different shifts over several days of operation. The table
below shows the results.

Sample	Tread Wear*			Average	Range
1	31	42	28	33.67	14
2	26	18	35	26.33	17
3	25	30	34	29.67	9
4	17	25	21	21.00	8
5	38	29	35	34.00	9
6	41	42	36	39.67	6
7	21	17	29	22.33	12
8	32	26	28	28.67	6
9	41	34	33	36.00	8
10	29	17	30	25.33	13
11	26	31	40	32.33	14
12	23	19	25	22.33	6
13	17	24	32	24.33	15
14	43	35	17	31.67	26
15	18	25	29	24.00	11
16	30	42	31	34.33	12
17	28	36	32	32.00	8
18	40	29	31	33.33	11
19	18	29	28	25.00	11
20	22	34	26	27.33	12

* Hundredths of an inch

After you have invoked the control chart for variables
template from the main menu, the following screen will appear:

```
A1: [W8]                                                              MENU
Data  Edit  Graph  Print  Main  Save  Clean  Quit
Enter data from samples
          A        B        C        D        E        F        G        H
1
2                       ===================================
3                       CONTROL CHART FOR VARIABLES
4                       ===================================
5
6
7
8     Problem _____Student Name:     _____
9
10
11    Number of observations..(M)..........................................
12
13    Number in each sample.....(n)................................ _____
14
15             D3                        X-Bar Chart          R-Chart
16             D4                     ----------------     ----------------
17             A2                         UCL  ___             UCL  ___
18             d2                         LCL  ___             LCL  ___
19                                    Mean X-Bar___         Mean R   ___
20
10-Feb-90  10:44 AM                         CMD
```

To begin, select DATA from the main menu. The template will prompt you for the problem title, your name, number of observations (samples), and number in each sample. Press the ENTER key after each response. After you have responded to these queries, the next screen will appear, in which you enter the observations for each sample.

Sample	Observations			Average	Range	UCL	LCL
	1	2	3				
1	31	42	28	33.67	14		
2	26	18	35	26.33	17		
3	25	30	34	29.67	9		
4	17	25	21	21.00	8		
5	38	29	35	34.00	9		
6	41	42	36	39.67	6		
7	21	17	29	22.33	12		
8	32	26	28	28.67	6		
9	41	34	33	36.00	8		
10	29	17	30	25.33	13		
11	26	31	40	32.33	14		
12	23	19	25	22.33	6		
13	17	24	32	24.33	15		
14	43	35	17	31.67	26		
15	18	25	29	24.00	11		
16	30	42	31	34.33	12		
17	28	36	32	32.00	8		
18	40	29	31	33.33	11		
19	18	29	28	25.00	11		
20	22	34	26	27.33	12		

The template will compute the sample averages and ranges, as well as the control limits.   These can be found by pressing the ENTER key once again to return to the first screen:

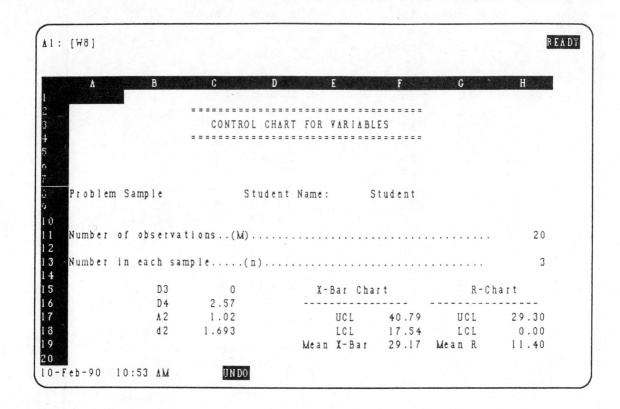

Additional Options:

1. From the EDIT submenu, you may make changes or corrections to the data. After you are satisfied with the changes, use ENTER key to return to the main menu of template commands.

2. Selecting the SAVE command enables you to save your file in another disk (other than the program diskette).

3.   The CLEAN command erases the current data, and you may invoke the DATA command to input another set of new data.

4. PRINT, MAIN, and QUIT commands serve the same purposes for all the templates.

5. GRAPH allows you to view the x-bar and R-charts. Examples of these charts are shown below.

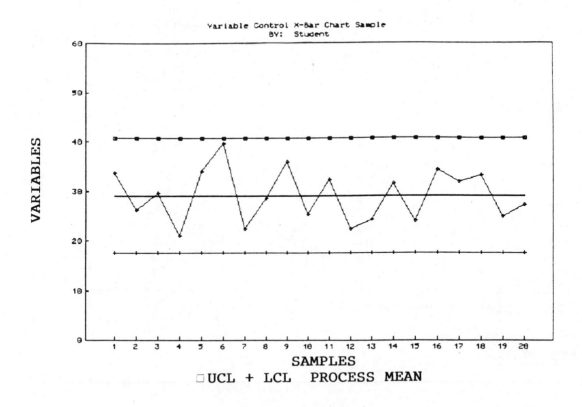

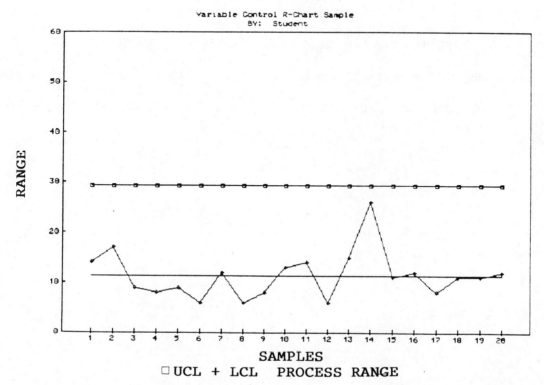

TEXT EXERCISES

1. Develop X-Bar and R-Charts for the following data:

			Observations		
Sample	1	2	3	4	5
1	3.05	3.08	3.07	3.11	3.11
2	3.13	3.07	3.05	3.10	3.10
3	3.06	3.04	3.12	3.11	3.10
4	3.09	3.08	3.09	3.09	3.07
5	3.10	3.06	3.06	3.07	3.08
6	3.08	3.10	3.13	3.03	3.06
7	3.06	3.06	3.08	3.10	3.08
8	3.11	3.08	3.07	3.07	3.07
9	3.09	3.09	3.08	3.07	3.09
10	3.06	3.11	3.07	3.09	3.07

(Chapter 19, problem 22, page 826)

CASE PROBLEM

Gotfryd Hydraulics, Inc., is a manufacturer of hydraulic machine tools. They have had a history of leakage trouble resulting from a certain critical fitting. Twenty-five samples of machined parts were selected, one per shift, and the diameter of the fitting was measured. The results are given in Table 1 below.

TABLE   1

	Diameter Measurement (cm) Observation			
Sample	1	2	3	4
1	10.94	10.64	10.88	10.70
2	10.66	10.66	10.68	10.68
3	10.68	10.68	10.62	10.68
4	10.03	10.42	10.48	11.06
5	10.70	10.46	10.76	10.80
6	10.38	10.74	10.62	10.54
7	10.46	10.90	10.52	10.74
8	10.66	10.04	10.58	11.04
9	10.50	10.44	10.74	10.66
10	10.58	10.64	10.60	10.26
11	10.80	10.36	10.60	10.22
12	10.42	10.36	10.72	10.68
13	10.52	10.70	10.62	10.58
14	11.04	10.58	10.42	10.36
15	10.52	10.40	10.60	10.40
16	10.38	10.02	10.60	10.60
17	10.56	10.68	10.78	10.34
18	10.58	10.50	10.48	10.60
19	10.42	10.74	10.64	10.50
20	10.48	10.44	10.32	10.70
21	10.56	10.78	10.46	10.42
22	10.82	10.64	11.00	10.01
23	10.28	10.46	10.82	10.84
24	10.64	10.56	10.92	10.54
25	10.84	10.68	10.44	10.68

a.   Construct control charts for this data ($D4 = 2.28$, $D3 = 0$, and $A2 = .73$ for $n = 25$).

b.   It was discovered that the regular machine operator was absent when samples 4, 8, 14, and 22 were taken. How will this affect the resutlts in part a?

c.   Table 2 represents measurements taken during the next 10 shifts.   What information does this provide to the quality-control manager ?

Table 2

Additional Sample	Observation			
	1	2	3	4
1	10.40	10.76	10.54	10.64
2	10.60	10.28	10.74	10.86
3	10.56	10.58	10.64	10.70
4	10.70	10.60	10.74	10.52
5	11.02	10.36	10.90	11.02
6	10.68	10.38	10.22	10.32
7	10.64	10.56	10.82	10.80
8	10.28	10.62	10.40	10.70
9	10.50	10.88	10.58	10.54
10	10.36	10.44	10.40	10.66

(Chapter 19, case problem, page 826)

SUPPLEMENTARY EXERCISES

1. A hydraulic press is used to form concrete blocks. There seems to be some concern over the lengths of the concrete blocks being stamped. A sample of ten blocks were measured and their lengths in inches found to be: 8.02, 8.06, 8.10, 8.15, 8.07, 7.95, 7.99, 8.11, 7.98, and 8.03. The press is set up to stamp an 8 inch concrete block. Construct a 3-sigma control limits, and identify if there are problems.

2. Shildar, Inc. manufactures cereals. Recently, customers were complaining about the variations in weights in the 24 ounce cereal boxes. A sample of ten boxes were measured and their weights in ounces found to be 23.2, 22.4, 24.1, 24.0, 24.2, 23.9, 24.5, 23.8, 22.4, and 22.8. The process

is set up to pour exactly 24 ounces of cereal in every box.

Construct 3-sigma control limits and

identify if there are problems.

3. In testing the resistance of a component used in a micro-

computer, the following data was obtained.

Sample	Observations		
1	414	388	402
2	408	382	406
3	396	402	392
4	390	398	362
5	398	442	436
6	400	400	414
7	444	390	410
8	430	372	362
9	376	398	382
10	342	400	402
11	400	402	384
12	408	414	388
13	382	430	400
14	402	409	400
15	399	424	413

Construct X-bar and R-charts for this data.   Determine if

the process is in control.   If not, eliminate any assignable

causes and compute revised limits.

4.   Develop X-bar and R-charts for the following data:

Sample	Observations				
1	3.05	3.08	3.07	3.11	3.11
2	3.13	3.07	3.05	3.10	3.10
3	3.06	3.04	3.12	3.11	3.10
4	3.09	3.08	3.09	3.09	3.07
5	3.10	3.06	3.06	3.07	3.08
6	3.08	3.10	3.13	3.03	3.06
7	3.06	3.06	3.08	3.10	3.08
8	3.11	3.08	3.07	3.07	3.07
9	3.09	3.09	3.08	3.07	3.09
10	3.06	3.11	3.07	3.09	3.07

Chapter 13
CONTROL CHART FOR ATTRIBUTES

Introduction

Attribute data assumes only two values, such as good or bad, pass or fail, and so on. Control charts for attributes are usually concerned with monitoring and controlling the fraction of nonconforming items. The type of control chart that is used is called a p-chart, where p represents the fraction of nonconforming items found in a sample. Control charts for attributes is discussed in Section 19.6 of the text.

Using the Control Chart for Attributes Template

To illustrate the use of the template, we will use the automated sorting machines in a post office example discussed in Section 19.6 of the text. The operators must read the zip code on a letter and divert the letter to the proper carrier route. Over 1 month's time, 25 samples of 100 letters were chosen and the number of errors were recorded. This is summarized in the following table.

Sample	Number of Errors	Sample	Number of Errors
1	3	7	3
2	1	8	6
3	0	9	1
4	0	10	4
5	2	11	0
6	5	12	2

Sample	Number of Errors	Sample	Number of Errors
13	1	14	3
15	4	16	1
17	1	18	2
19	5	20	2
21	3	22	4
23	1	24	0
25	1		

The fraction defective in each sample is simply the number of errors divided by 100. Adding the fraction defectives and dividing by 25 yields p-bar = .55/25 = .022. The standard deviation (S p-bar) is .01467.

After you have invoked the control chart for attributes template from the main menu, the following screen will appear:

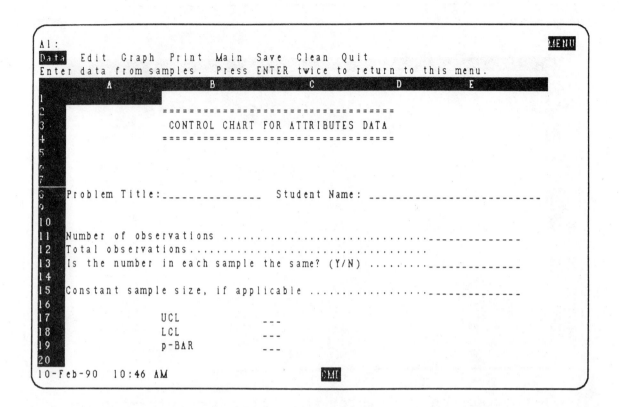

To begin, select DATA from the main menu. The template will prompt you for the problem title, your name, and the number of observations. Press the ENTER key after each response. Respond to the sample size and whether the number in each sample the same. After completing this screen, the following screen will appear:

```
C34: U [W16]                                                              READY

                A            B           C            D            E
31                        CONTROL CHART by ATTRIBUTE
32                          Sample        Number                 Fraction
33          Sample          Size      Nonconforming          Nonconforming
34            1             100                                    0.0000
35            2             100                                    0.0000
36            3             100                                    0.0000
37            4             100                                    0.0000
38            5             100                                    0.0000
39            6             100                                    0.0000
40            7             100                                    0.0000
41            8             100                                    0.0000
42            9             100                                    0.0000
43           10             100                                    0.0000
44                        ------        -----
45                          1000           0
46       Press "ENTER" to return to the main menu.
47       Number of                Average Nonconforming =         0.0000
48       Standard                 Standard Deviation =            0.0000
49       Deviations               Upper Control Limit =           0.0000
50            3                   Lower Control Limit =           0.0000
10-Feb-90  10:47 AM                        CMT
```

In this screen, you enter the number nonconforming for each sample. Control chart parameters are shown on the lower portion of the screen and on the intial screen as well.

Additional Options:

1.   From the DATA submenu, you may select NEW DATA or EXTEND-DATA or MAIN.   These selections will enable you to enter the new data, extend data, and let's you return to the main menu.

2.   Additionally, EDIT, GRAPH, SAVE, AND CLEAN options are available.

TEXT EXERCISES

1. The fraction nonconforming for an automotive piston is given

    below for 20 samples. Two hundred units are inspected each

    day. Construct a p-chart and interpret the results.

Sample	Fraction Nonconforming	Sample	Fraction Nonconfor.
1	.04	11	.07
2	.05	12	.09
3	.03	13	.05
4	.02	14	.04
5	.02	15	.03
6	.04	16	.04
7	.04	17	.03
8	.06	18	.05
9	.04	19	.02
10	.08	20	.04

2. One hundred insurance claim forms are inspected daily over

    25 working days and the number of forms with errors are as

    recorded. Construct a p-chart. If any points occur outside

    the control limits, assume that assignable causes have been

    determined. Then construct a revised chart.

Day	Number Nonconforming	Day	Number Nonconforming
1	2	14	2
2	1	15	1
3	2	16	3
4	3	17	4
5	0	18	0
6	2	19	0
7	0	20	1
8	2	21	0
9	7	22	2
10	1	23	8
11	3	24	2
12	0	25	1
13	0		

(Chapter 19, problem 18, page 825)

SUPPLEMENTARY EXERCISES

1. The fraction defective for an automotive piston is given below for 20 samples. Two hundred units are inspected each day. Construct a p-chart and interpret the results.

Sample	Fraction Defective	Sample	Fraction Defective
1	0.11	11	0.16
2	0.16	12	0.23
3	0.12	13	0.15
4	0.10	14	0.12
5	0.09	15	0.11
6	0.12	16	0.11
7	0.12	17	0.14
8	0.15	18	0.16
9	0.09	19	0.10
10	0.13	20	0.13

2. Samples of size 100 have been randomly selected during each shift of 25 shifts in a production process. The data is given below. Construct a p-chart and determine if the process is in control. If not, eliminate any data points that appear to be due to assignable causes and construct a new chart.

Sample	# of Defectives	Sample	# of Defectives
1	10	14	16
2	14	15	13
3	22	16	18
4	17	17	20
5	27	18	23
6	42	19	27
7	49	20	59
8	36	21	52
9	17	22	25
10	20	23	16
11	35	24	45
12	39	25	68
13	12		

3. MARKAL industries had been faced with a severe quality problems. Following data were obtained when 10 samples of their core product were analyzed.

Sample Number	# of Defects in sample
1	3
2	2
3	5
4	7
5	1
6	2
7	0
8	1
9	0
10	3

a.   Construct a p-chart for this data.

b.   Management observed five additional samples:

Sample Number	Number of Defects
1	4
2	0
3	6
4	5
5	1

Based on this evidence, do you conclude that the process is in control? If not, explain.